Readers Respond
All Will Be Well

If you have faith it will strengthen it. If you have no faith it will give you some. *I really enjoyed this book.* With more heart-provoking questions, clear summary statements to hold on to, and new perspectives as you read true stories, this book will give you a new peace about having faith in God. You'll definitely want your favorite yummy treat and a hi-lighter for this gratifying yet life-changing read.

—DANIELLE A., SURREY, UK

Your Amazing Book. Glowingly positive!

This is a truly beautiful book: kudos! You reduced me to tears a few times, but mostly it just felt affirmatory and challenging (in a good way)! Have copied a few bits that really spoke to me in the P.S. I also find it a very hope-filled book. It would, I think, encourage people new to faith as well as strengthen those of us who've been working on our faith for a while. It's a deeply thoughtful, well-researched book.

I knew that Daniel has been called fictional, but I never read that he must have been very old during his hour of trial. I also love the way that you point the ending of each chapter with questions, directly to the reader. You also have a happy knack of finding just the right punchline from Scripture for your point.

P.S. Favorite bits at the moment:

"When the outcome of our struggles feels disappointing, this can place great strain on our faith. It requires trust in God at the highest level to release our expectations. This aspect of faith is probably one of the hardest for us to fully embrace. We need the discernment of the Holy Spirit to recognize that *God's highest priority is to transform us, not just our circumstances.*"

—ALICE M., KENT, UK

Wow! This book is what I needed
To remind me to never give up.

The stories of seemingly insignificant people in the Bible whom we hardly remember—Jochebed, Miriam, Hananiah, Mishael, Azariah, the Shunammite woman, Jairus, Blind Bartimaeus, the Canaanite woman, the Centurion, the four friends who raised the roof, the hemorrhaging woman—how they have displayed extraordinary faith and therefore were extremely rewarded!

The stories of these people were examined and broken down for us to fully understand what they did and how their actions were rewarded with tremendous blessings. It gave us examples of actions to follow and emulate to inspire us to do the same! The seemingly insignificant role of Jochebed in the great exodus of Israelites from Egypt was magnified in this book, reminding us that a role is never too small or insignificant.

In turn, the author reminded us that even great people in the Bible, like Peter and David, can mess up and fail, but how God turns it all around once they have repented. I can't wait to share it with friends and family who need to be reminded of how simple faith can literally move mountains!

—MRS. DE DIOS O., NEVADA, USA

This is a very inspiring book.

It's one thing to know about faith, but this book embraces all the aspects of faith and brings it to life. It inspired me to see God and faith in Him in a whole new way. I highly recommend this book,

Contents

Chapter Seven

Chapter Eight

Chapter Nine

Chapter Ten

Chapter Eleven

Chapter Twelve

Chapter Thirteen

Chapter Fourteen

Prologue

This verse inspired me to write this book.

"Tell the godly that all will be well for them. They will enjoy the rich reward they have earned!"

—ISAIAH 3:10 (*NEW LIVING TRANSLATION*)

Chapter One

"LORD, PLEASE LET
IT BE A GIRL!"

What, then, shall we say in response to these things?
If God is for us, who can be against us?

—ROMANS 8:31 (*NEW INTERNATIONAL VERSION*)

The sounds of wailing women had already replaced the singing of lullabies in Goshen. Every pregnant woman was also praying a very strange prayer: "Lord, please let my baby be a girl." Nine months is a very long time to wait for a baby to be born, and most people usually take that time to make very careful preparations. But cribs, formulas, and nurseries were the furthest things from the young parents' minds as they waited anxiously for the longed-for births. A once-bustling city, urgent with people and activity, Goshen was instead filled with anxiety and fear. The nervousness was palpable, as anxiety levels rose.

So what on earth was going on? Why the passionate—universal—desire to give birth only to daughters? And why were these expectant mothers all making the same passion-ate plea to God?

This is why: because every newborn male faced certain death. At the birth of each male, the distraught parents could hardly contain their pain. They wept until they could weep no more. Cries and lamentations filled the air. Goshen's residents desperately needed a miracle. Powerless to change their own horrific circumstances, everyone cried aloud to God.

To uncover the cause of this calamity a brief history will be needed. This will help us to discover how things got to this point. Pharaoh was troubled by some disturb-ing dreams.

So he called for all the magicians and wise men of Egypt. When Pharaoh told them his dreams, not one of them could tell him what they meant.

Finally, the king's chief cupbearer spoke up. "Today I have been reminded of my failure," he told Pharaoh. "Some time ago, you were angry with the chief baker and me, and you imprisoned us in the palace of the captain of the guard. One night the chief baker and I each had a dream, and each dream had its own meaning.

"There was a young Hebrew man with us in the prison who was a slave of the captain of the guard. We told him our dreams, and he told us what each of our dreams meant. And everything happened just as he had predicted. I was restored to my position as cupbearer, and the chief baker was executed and impaled on a pole."

Pharaoh sent for Joseph at once, and he was quickly brought from the prison. After he shaved and changed his clothes, he went in and stood before Pharaoh. Then Pharaoh said to Joseph, "I had a dream last night, and no one here can tell me what it means. But I have heard that when you hear about a dream you can interpret it."

"It is beyond my power to do this," Joseph replied. "But God can tell you what it means and set you at ease."

So Pharaoh told Joseph his dream. "In my dream," he said, "I was standing on the bank of the Nile River, and I saw seven fat, healthy cows come up out of the river and begin grazing in the marsh grass. But then I saw seven sick-looking cows, scrawny and thin, come up after them. I've never seen such sorry-looking animals in all the land of Egypt. These thin, scrawny cows ate the seven fat cows. But afterward you wouldn't have known it, for they were still as thin and scrawny as before! Then I woke up.

"In my dream I also saw seven heads of grain, full and beautiful, growing on a single stalk. Then seven more heads of grain appeared, but these were blighted, shriveled, and withered by the east wind. And the shriveled heads swallowed the seven healthy heads. I told these dreams to the magicians, but no one could tell me what they mean."

Joseph responded, "Both of Pharaoh's dreams mean the same thing. God is telling Pharaoh in advance what he is about to do. The seven healthy cows and the seven healthy heads of grain both represent seven years of prosperity. The seven thin, scrawny cows that came up later and the seven thin heads of grain, withered by the east wind, represent seven years of famine.

"This will happen just as I have described it, for God has revealed to Pharaoh in advance what he is about to do. The next seven years will be a period of great prosperity throughout the land of Egypt. But afterward there will be seven years of famine so great that all the prosperity will be forgotten in Egypt. Famine will destroy the land. This famine will be so severe that even the memory of the good years will be erased.

"As for having two similar dreams, it means that these events have been decreed by God, and he will soon make them happen. Therefore, Pharaoh should find an intelligent and wise man and put him in charge of the entire land of Egypt. Then Pharaoh should appoint supervisors over the land and let them collect one-fifth of all the crops during the seven good years. Have them gather all the food produced in the good years that are just ahead and bring it to Pharaoh's storehouses. Store it away, and guard it so there will be food in the cities. That way there will be enough to eat when the seven years of famine come to the land of Egypt. Otherwise this famine will destroy the land."

Joseph's suggestions were well received by Pharaoh and his officials. So Pharaoh asked his officials, "Can we find anyone else like this man so obviously filled with the spirit of God?" Then Pharaoh said to Joseph, "Since God has revealed the meaning of the dreams to you, clearly no one else is as intelligent or wise as you are. You will be in charge of my court, and all my people will take orders from you. Only I, sitting on my throne, will have a rank higher than yours."

Pharaoh said to Joseph, "I hereby put you in charge of the entire land of Egypt." Then Pharaoh removed his signet ring from his hand and placed it on Joseph's finger. He dressed him in fine linen clothing and hung a gold chain around his neck. Then he had Joseph ride in the chariot reserved for his second-in-command. And wherever Joseph went, the command was shouted, "Kneel down!" So Pharaoh put Joseph in charge of all Egypt. And Pharaoh said to him, "I am Pharaoh, but no one will lift a hand or foot in the entire land of Egypt without your approval."

Then Pharaoh gave Joseph a new Egyptian name, Zaphenath-paneah. He also gave him a wife, whose name was Asenath. She was the daughter of Potiphera, the priest of On. So Joseph took charge of the entire land of Egypt. He was thirty years old when he began serving in the court of Pharaoh, the king of Egypt . . .

As predicted, for seven years the land produced bumper crops. During those years, Joseph gathered all the crops grown in Egypt and stored the grain from the surrounding fields in the cities. He piled up huge amounts of grain like sand on the seashore. Finally, he stopped keeping records because there was too much to measure (Genesis 41:8–49, NLT).

At last the seven years of bumper crops throughout the land of Egypt came to an end. Then the seven years of famine began, just as Joseph had predicted. The famine also struck all the surrounding countries, but throughout Egypt there was plenty of food. Eventually, however, the famine spread throughout the land of Egypt as well. And when the people cried out to Pharaoh for food, he told them, "Go to Joseph, and do whatever he tells you." So with severe famine everywhere, Joseph opened up the storehouses and distributed grain to the Egyptians, for the famine was severe throughout the land of Egypt. And people from all around came to Egypt to buy grain from Joseph because the famine was severe throughout the world.

When Jacob heard that grain was available in Egypt, he said to his sons, "Why are you standing around looking at one another? I have heard there is grain in Egypt. Go down there, and buy enough grain to keep us alive. Otherwise we'll die." So Joseph's ten older brothers went down to Egypt to buy grain (Genesis 41:53–42:3, NLT).

Since Joseph was governor of all Egypt and in charge of selling grain to all the people, it was to him that his brothers came. When they arrived, they bowed before him, with their faces to the ground. Joseph recognized his brothers instantly . . . [but] they did not recognize him (Genesis 42:6–8, NLT).

"I am Joseph!" he said to his brothers. "Is my father still alive?" But his brothers were speechless! They were stunned to realize that Joseph was standing there in front of them. "Please, come closer," he said to them. So they came closer. And he said again, "I am Joseph, your brother, whom you sold into slavery in Egypt. But don't be upset, and don't be angry with yourselves for selling me to this place. It was God who sent me here ahead of you to preserve your lives. This famine that has ravaged the land for two years will last five more years, and there will be neither plowing nor harvesting. God has sent me ahead of you to keep you and your families alive and to preserve many survivors. So it was God who sent me here, not you! And he is the one who made me an adviser to Pharaoh—the manager of his entire palace and the governor of all Egypt.

"Now hurry back to my father and tell him, 'this is what your son Joseph says: God has made me master over all the land of Egypt. So come down to me immediately! You can live in the region of Goshen, where you can be near me with all your children and grandchildren, your flocks and herds, and everything you own. I will take care of you there, for there are still five years of famine ahead of us. Otherwise you, your household, and all your animals will starve'" (Genesis 45:3–11, NLT).

So Jacob left Beersheba, and his sons took him to Egypt. They carried him and their little ones and their wives in the wagons Pharaoh had provided for them.

They also took all their livestock and all the personal belongings they had acquired in the land of Canaan. So Jacob and his entire family went to Egypt—sons and grandsons, daughters and granddaughters—all his descendants (Genesis 46:5–7, NLT).

And Joseph said to his brothers and to his father's entire family, "I will go to Pharaoh and tell him, 'my brothers and my father's entire family have come to me from the land of Canaan. "'These men are shepherds, and they raise livestock. They have brought with them their flocks and herds and everything they own.'"

Then he said, "When Pharaoh calls for you and asks you about your occupation, you must tell him, 'We, your servants, have raised livestock all our lives, as our ancestors have always done.' When you tell him this, he will let you live here in the region of Goshen, for the Egyptians despise shepherds" (Genesis 46:31–34, NLT).

Then Pharaoh said to Joseph, "Now that your father and brothers have joined you here, choose any place in the entire land of Egypt for them to live. Give them the best land of Egypt. Let them live in the region of Goshen. And if any of them have special skills, put them in charge of my livestock too." Then Joseph brought in his father, Jacob, and presented him to Pharaoh. And Jacob blessed Pharaoh (Genesis 47:5–7, NLT).

Meanwhile, the famine became so severe that all the food was used up, and people were starving throughout the lands of Egypt and Canaan. By selling grain to the people, Joseph eventually collected all the money in Egypt and Canaan, and he put the money in Pharaoh's treasury (Genesis 47:13–14, NLT). So Joseph bought all the land of Egypt for Pharaoh (Genesis 47:20, NLT).

Meanwhile, the people of Israel settled in the region of Goshen in Egypt. There they acquired property, and they were fruitful, and their population grew rapidly. (Genesis 47:27–28, NLT).

These are the names of the sons of Israel (that is, Jacob) who moved to Egypt with their father, each with his family: Reuben, Simeon, Levi, Judah, Issachar, Zebulun, Benjamin, Dan, Naphtali, Gad, and Asher. In all, Jacob had seventy descendants in Egypt, including Joseph, who was already there.

In time, Joseph and all of his brothers died, ending that entire generation. But their descendants, the Israelites, had many children and grandchildren. In fact, they multiplied so greatly that they became extremely powerful and filled the land.

Eventually, a new king came to power in Egypt who knew nothing about Joseph or what he had done. He said to his people, "Look, the people of Israel now outnumber us and are stronger than we are. We must make a plan to keep them from growing even more. If we don't and if war breaks out, they will join our enemies and fight against us. Then they will escape from the country."

So the Egyptians made the Israelites their slaves. They appointed brutal slave drivers over them, hoping to wear them down with crushing labor. They forced them to build the cities of Pithom and Rameses as supply centers for the king. But the more the Egyptians oppressed them, the more the Israelites multiplied and spread, and the more alarmed the Egyptians became. So the Egyptians worked the people of Israel without mercy. They made their lives bitter, forcing them to mix mortar and make bricks and do all the work in the fields. They were ruthless in all their demands.

Then Pharaoh, the king of Egypt, gave this order to the Hebrew midwives, Shiphrah and Puah: "When you help the Hebrew women as they give birth, watch as they deliver. If the baby is a boy, kill him; if it is a girl, let her live." But because the midwives feared God, they refused to obey the king's orders. They allowed the boys to live, too (Exodus 1:1–17, NLT).

Then Pharaoh gave this order to all his people: "Throw every newborn Hebrew boy into the Nile River. But you may let the girls live" (Exodus 1:22, NLT; more can be found in Genesis chapters 37 and 39–47).

Joseph's ingenious plan rescued Egypt, and his wisdom boosted Pharaoh's royal coffers to unheard-of levels. In fact, Egypt continued to prosper long after the famine was history. Many surrounding nations were also blessed by the young Hebrew's insight. Joseph had proven himself to be a godsend to Egypt; and his people—the Hebrews, sometimes called the Israelites—settled in the land of Goshen, contributing greatly to Egypt's wealth.

When the new pharaoh came to power, he appeared to neither know nor care about the recent past and viewed the Hebrews as a security threat, attempting to annihilate their people. Of course, ignorance of history can pose a threat to freedom in any society. And all too often, to quote a famous adage, "No good deed goes unpunished."

Even worse, all power and influence were on Pharaoh's side. It's impossible to imagine the anguish of parents, after enduring all the pain and trauma of giving birth to a child, only to watch their newborn taken away and murdered. So what should we do when God seems deaf to all prayers and unwilling to intervene even in such appalling circumstances? What would you have done had you been a pregnant Hebrew in Goshen?

The Scriptures tell us that anyone in trouble should call on God for help, and the Israelites might also have recalled similar words of guidance to these:

> Call on me when you are in trouble, and I will rescue you, and you will give me glory (Psalm 50:15, NLT).

> Anyone among you in trouble? Let them pray (James 5:13, NIV).

Now, the Israelites had a very special relationship with God. For them, worshipping Him was no empty exercise. Their faith had been passed down to them by their forefathers—Abraham, Isaac, and Jacob—and was central to their identity. They knew that God existed and that He could save them from this terrible ordeal, so Goshen's residents cried out to God for help.

> "I am the God of your fathers—the God of Abraham, the God of Isaac, and the God of Jacob . . . . I have certainly seen the oppression of my people in Egypt. I have heard their cries of distress because of their harsh slave drivers. Yes, I am aware of their suffering" (Exodus 3:6–7, NLT).

Yet Pharaoh remained obdurate. Hope of divine rescue faded from many Hebrew hearts. Can you imagine how angry God must have been when He saw the brutal treatment of His people? Although the Egyptians didn't acknowledge the God of Israel, He had still been very kind to them: forewarning them about the natural disaster and even providing them with a young Hebrew leader to guide them through their crisis.

Without the protection that Joseph's wisdom had brought to Egypt, the nation would have been wiped out by the years of famine. The depths of the misery being experienced by Joseph's descendants would have been utterly unimaginable, either to Joseph or to the previous Pharaoh.

Amidst all this turmoil, "A man and woman from the tribe of Levi got married. The woman became pregnant and gave birth to a son" (Exodus 2:1–2, NLT). The names of the couple were Jochebed and Amram and, when this verse was written, they already had two children, with Aaron aged three, and Miriam about ten or twelve. (See Numbers 26:59, Exodus 6:20, and Exodus 7:7.)

In those terrible days, neither Jochebed nor her husband would have wanted their next child to be a boy. A newborn male—at least in their city, at that time—had no future. His survival chances resembled the proverbial snowball's chance in hell. Aaron had escaped—having been born long before the killings had begun—but imagine the couple's distress when their newest son arrived!

All hopes of another girl dashed, nothing short of a miracle could save Moses from imminent death. What a terrifying moment for his poor parents! They must have felt absolutely hunted. "What do we do now?" must have been their first thought. What used to be the happiest of events, the birth of a longed-for child, had become the most horrific occasion imaginable.

Before Pharaoh's edict, a son who could carry on the family name had been considered perhaps the greatest of God's blessings. As things stood, there was no worse time to have a son. No sonograms were available—of course!—so it was an agonizing wait for each expectant parent. Even families to whom baby girls had been given couldn't rejoice; instead, they had to comfort their grieving neighbors. Before her own baby arrived, Jochebed had probably witnessed newborns being snatched from their screaming parents. And there were many of these: the Hebrews had many children, because God had blessed them. "The more the Egyptians oppressed them, the more the Israelites multiplied and spread" (Exodus 1:12, NLT).

So what could Jochebed do? Her family was powerless. Not even an Egyptian could have escaped Pharaoh's law. As Hebrews, Jochebed and her husband had no hope at all. Yet this couple still—even after so many centuries—are able to teach us that having an unshakeable faith in God is not only for those enjoying lives of ease and plenty but is achievable even during the very darkest times.

Because God was already powerfully at work: He was about to show His people how to triumph over evil. Jochebed and Amram would soon become "hall of faith" heroes, something that started the moment they took their first courageous step toward saving their son.

And when she saw that he was [especially] beautiful and healthy, she hid him for three months [to protect him from the Egyptians] (Exodus 2:2, *Amplified Bible*).

By faith Moses' parents hid him for three months after he was born because they saw he

was no ordinary child, and they were not afraid
of the king's edict (Hebrews 11:23, NIV).

This swift action right after their son's birth proved
to be a life-saving miracle, not only for their son but
their entire nation! Here's the first lesson that we can
take from this:

> *Just because you don't have all the answers to a*
> *problem doesn't mean that you should do nothing.*

Although only a temporary measure—in that delaying their child's death was perhaps the best that they
could hope for—at least this small, brave step increased
their baby's life span by three months. Basically, while
every other infant boy perished, Jochebed and Amram
gained time—time to seek further guidance and wisdom
from God.

Of course, they had no possible way of knowing that
Moses would survive, but life still remains the most precious gift that we can possess. So—as much as it might
be within our own power—it's up to us to lessen the negative impact of our own circumstances. While there's even a
single hope of keeping someone alive, we must do all that
we can. Because death is final: it's spilled water that can't
be gathered back—unless God's sovereignty intervenes
in order to reverse it.

Like water spilled on the ground, which cannot be recovered, so we must die (2 Samuel 14:14, NIV).

There is hope only for the living. As they say, "It's better to be a live dog than a dead lion!" (Ecclesiastes 9:4, NLT).

Handing their baby over to the authorities would have meant that nothing further could possibly be done to save his life. Although their child could not remain hidden forever, this first courageous step paved the way for God to work greater miracles in the future. "The prudent sees danger and hides himself, but the simple go on and suffer for it" (Proverbs 27:12, *English Standard Version*).

Never give up faith in God.

Continue to search for viable options to fight, even in what might appear to be a hopeless situation. An illustration of this can be daily drawn from every hospital emergency room. When a desperately ill person is rushed in, the medical staff very rarely has every detail of the patient's health history. Instead, they use their experience and expertise to stabilize the patient's *current* condition, before checking out the underlying issues.

So if you're in trouble, first take every measure possible to lessen the negative circumstances of your situation, while continuing to seek God's wisdom. Second,

Continue to evaluate the situation and—although
your current options may appear hugely limited—
remember that smaller victories can pave
the way for far bigger ones.

While it may seem to us as if God is doing nothing about our urgent needs, He is always at work. "Jesus replied, "My Father is always working, and so am I" (John 5:17, NLT).

Jochebed and Amram had an epic battle before them, and their initial actions probably felt woefully inadequate. Yet as we read earlier, the Scriptures confirm that it was their faith that gave them the courage to hide their son. If you ever find yourself facing what feels like an impossible situation, don't be paralyzed into inaction or allow yourself to cave in to your fears. Instead, remember Jochebed and Amram's courage, exercise every ounce of faith that you possess, and initiate any steps that you can think of, whether big or small, with even the smallest chance of leading you out of your crisis.

Trust in God more than in your negative circumstances.

We need to exercise the faith that we already have in order to receive God's grace, to grow a still stronger faith, and to uproot deep-seated problems. Someone once showed me some mustard seeds in a small cup. They were *minute!*—smaller than the tiniest grains of rice. But when planted these can grow to become "some of the largest" of garden plants. Equally, even the tiniest measure of faith—one the size of the least-impressive grain—can grow to be truly powerful.

> The kingdom of heaven is like a mustard seed, which a man took and planted in his field. Though it is the smallest of all seeds, yet when it grows, it is the largest of garden plants and becomes a tree, so that the birds come and perch in its branches (Matthew 13:31–32, NIV).

> And the Lord said, "If you had faith like a grain of mustard seed, you could say to this mulberry tree, 'Be uprooted and planted in the sea,' and it would obey you" (Luke 17:6, ESV).

> Do not despise these small beginnings, for the LORD rejoices to see the work begin" (Zechariah 4:10, NLT).

Your own fight will probably be completely remote from Jochebed and Amram's (e.g., hospital visit, business challenge, family issue, etc.) but, just like them, you should never give up on your faith. Run to God for cover and fight to the very end—even if the fight takes you longer than you had hoped for, or believed that you could endure.

The name of the LORD is a strong tower; the righteous man runs into it and is safe (Proverbs 18:10, ESV).

Fight the good fight of the faith (1 Timothy 6:12, NIV).

Do you want to be shown that faith without actions is useless? (James 2:20, *Good News Translation*).

The fight of faith is called "the good fight" because we will always be victorious, as long as we abide in God's love, wisdom, and power. After all, He has already accomplished victory over all evil on humanity's behalf.

The reason the Son of God appeared was to destroy the devil's work" (1 John 3:8, NIV).

"I have told you these things, so that in me you may have peace. In this world you will have trouble. But take heart! I have overcome the world" (John 16:33, NIV).

Jochebed and Amram never knew that the final outcome of their decision would be a mighty movement of God in Egypt. But they held tightly to their faith in the face of a great trial, and, to this day, they continue to inspire us. Miraculous turnarounds are possible whenever God is involved, as long as we place our faith in Him.

So, inspired by Jochebed and Amram, I recommend that you invite God into your own desperate situation and fully exercise your faith. For He is always faithful. "Nothing will be impossible with God" Luke 1:37, ESV).

Later, we'll touch on what the correct response should be when our longed-for miracle fails to happen. Should we release all our faith, simply because we can only see the rough and jagged side of the beautiful tapestry that God is weaving? No, instead we need to dig our "faith heels" in and fight for our and our loved ones' lives!

Remember: God has an individual destiny for every single human being on our planet. The fulfillment of your personal destiny begins with trust in our loving Creator.

Is anything too hard for the LORD? (Genesis 18:14, NIV).

Chapter Two

"Will I Ever See You Again?"

*The LORD says, "I will guide you along
the best pathway for your life. I will
advise you and watch over you."*

—Psalm 32:8 (NLT)

Even for a woman as brave as Jochebed, the three months spent hiding Moses must have been one of the most stressful periods of her life. I have no idea what she told her neighbors. Everyone must surely have wondered which gender of child she had given birth to—or whether it had died in the womb. Newborns and their gender were probably the hottest topics for discussion at the time, and some of Jochebed's friends might well have been grieving their own losses (which might have made them hesitate to ask her, of course).

It's often said that misery loves company. Jochebed's neighbors may have been really interested in what was going on in her home, or they may just have been in search of comfort. At any rate, the three months probably crawled by, while our faith heroine must have rung heaven's 911 emergency line off the hook! In the meantime, Pharaoh's command stood firm and this fearless woman constantly wondered what to do next.

You might have thought that after their powerful display of faith in Him, God would have moved swiftly to assist Jochebed and Amram. But as time went by, no supernatural signs appeared, as had been the case with Mary, mother of Jesus, for example. Mary was visited by one of God's angelic messengers, who confirmed the astonishing things that were about to take place in her life. (See Luke 1:26–38.) This supernatural visitation must have boosted Mary's faith and given her immense courage to persevere. Yet with Jochebed and her family, there were no supernatural signs. The family had to demonstrate their extraordinary faith with no miracles to lean on—unless, of course, you count the fact that successfully hiding their infant son for those three months was already a huge miracle from God!

But this impressive couple had more faith
in God's ability to save their son than
in the enemy's ability to harm him.

Great courage often lies quietly in the hearts of the least-esteemed people—in this case, in people who were slaves. Jochebed's is a powerful example for us to follow, because we too need to hold tightly to our faith in the face of adversity. Her actions were not a denial of her dire situation; instead, they were a faith-filled resistance against the evil that threatened to destroy her son.

> The LORD is my light and my salvation—so why should I be afraid? The LORD is my fortress, protecting me from danger, so why should I tremble? (Psalm 27:1, NLT).

> They who wait for the LORD shall renew their strength; they shall mount up with wings like eagles; they shall run and not be weary; they shall walk and not faint (Isaiah 40:31, ESV).

Jochebed and her family basically gave us all a masterclass on *what to do when you don't really know what to do!* While groping through what must have felt like total darkness, Jochebed chose to stay on course. Our soon to be "faith hall of famer" displayed such wonderful faith and reliance upon God, that she challenges us to do the same.

As time went on, Jochebed's baby grew too big—and possibly too loud—to hide. They couldn't hide him forever. His mother had to come up with a new plan of action.

When she could no longer hide him, she got a basket made of papyrus reeds and waterproofed it with tar and pitch. She put the baby in the basket and laid it among the reeds along the bank of the Nile. The baby's sister then stood at a distance, watching to see what would happen to him. Soon, Pharaoh's daughter came down to bathe in the river, and her attendants walked along the riverbank. When the princess saw the basket among the reeds, she sent her maid to get it for her. When the princess opened it, she saw the baby. The little boy was crying, and she felt sorry for him. "This must be one of the Hebrew children," she said.

Then the baby's sister approached the princess. "Should I go and find one of the Hebrew women to nurse the baby for you?" she asked.

"Yes, do!" the princess replied.

So the girl went and called the baby's mother. "Take this baby and nurse him for me," the princess told the baby's mother. "I will pay you for your help." So Jochebed took her baby home and nursed him. Later, when the boy was older, his mother took him back to Pharaoh's daughter, who adopted him as her own son. The princess named him Moses for, she explained, "I lifted him out of the water" (Exodus 2:3–10, NLT).

Wow! What a completely amazing turn of events! I can only imagine Jochebed's feelings when she took what she probably believed would be her last look at her child, placed him in the homemade basket and pushed him out onto the wild and scary Nile. That basket could so easily have simply become the little boy's coffin! Nothing but trust in God could have strengthened her. How desperate she must have felt as she watched her baby drift away on the water. Did she wait to watch or did she rush away quickly so as not to see him drown? How desperately she must have prayed in that moment!

So many bad things could have happened to Moses. Topping the list would have been Pharaoh's soldiers spotting him, instead of the princess. He'd have been killed within seconds. The second-worst, probably: the Nile's hungry crocodiles. Neither of these terrible outcomes was preventable. But his faith-filled mother still dared to release her son into God's hands, wondering, "Will I ever see you again?" Here is another important lesson to ponder, while waiting for God to answer our own prayers.

Although God may appear to be doing nothing about our dire and urgent needs, He may actually be working on greater miracles than the miracles that we're asking for.

Our planet, and everything in it, was created by God. He is fully at work behind the scenes, doing good things for human beings—far more than we could either ask Him for or (in some cases) even imagine. Even if God were to share why He sometimes does things in the ways that He does, we would probably *still* not be able to comprehend His ways.

> "My thoughts are nothing like your thoughts," says the LORD. "And my ways are far beyond anything you could imagine. For just as the heavens are higher than the earth, so my ways are higher than your ways and my thoughts higher than your thoughts" (Isaiah 55:8–9, NLT).

God did not disappoint Jochebed. Instead, He revealed His power through one of the very few humans with the power and resources to protect her baby: the Egyptian Princess. Within just a few hours of wondering whether she would ever see her son again and trying not to imagine all the terrible things that might be happening to him, Jochebed was once again holding her son in her arms, being paid to nurse him as a member of Pharaoh's household! A real miracle!

It was also a mighty victory for the family. Jochebed could never have known what the final outcome of her faith would be; instead she had simply prayed to God for a rescue. And it was God who had orchestrated every event, teaching us that we should place unshakeable faith in Him, even under the most terrifying circumstances.

It was God who made sure that everyone was where they were supposed to be—and *when* they were supposed to be there. The timing was *beyond* impressive. Imagine it:

what if the princess had decided not to go out that day, or had chosen to venture, not to the river, but to the market instead? What if she had been taken ill or if some minor mishap—a mistake from one of her attendants, perhaps—had prevented her from being at the riverside at the same time as Moses? So many *what ifs*! Yet God needed the Egyptian princess to be at that very spot at that very moment, and He ensured that she was. "Indeed, he who watches over Israel never slumbers or sleeps" (Psalm 121:4, NLT).

While many people in Goshen would have been thinking that they were the ones waiting for God to move, instead He was already powerfully at work through the efforts of a humble slave couple, who had produced the deliverer of their entire nation. The events of that day must have surpassed the wildest hopes of the family's prayers.

In terms of ourselves, this should serve as a reminder that God never fails. We need to place our absolute trust in Him. Our Creator cares for all His creation—humans especially. We can rest assured that He is watching over us and orchestrating every single thing in our lives, in order to work them together for good. "And we know that God causes everything to work together for the good of those who love God and are called according to his purpose for them" (Romans 8:28, NLT).

The way in which Jochebed behaved serves as a guide to exercising unshakeable faith. Here's another important lesson for us to draw from this faith heroine:

*Great miracles from God are rarely achieved in one
big step. They may occur in a series of small steps.
Take things one day, and one step, at a time.*

Another noteworthy point is that Jochebed's name
in Hebrew means "God's glory." But her life, as we know,
was very far from being glorious. Instead, she and everyone she cared for was a slave, subjected daily to Egyptian
brutality. Really, any impartial onlooker might well have
wrongly concluded that God didn't care about Jochebed
at all. Her life and experiences certainly didn't match up
with God's glory. Instead, her circumstances made it seem
as if Jochebed had been given the wrong name, lived in the
worst possible place, and been born at entirely the wrong
time in history.

Yet God had different ideas. God made the meaning
of Jochebed's name a prophetic statement through which
He chose

to reveal His glory. Although the citizens of Goshen
appeared to have no hope, Jochebed and her family's
unwavering faith soon turned things around—not only
for her but also for her people. She proved that no matter
how small or inadequate our own actions may appear
compared to the size of our struggles, we must let God
ignite the light of hope in our hearts that will lead us
towards a fuller faith in Him. Even the tiniest measure
of faith can be sufficient to move mountains.

"Truly I tell you, if you have faith as small as a mustard seed, you can say to this mountain, 'Move from here to there,' and it will move. Nothing will be impossible for you"(Matthew 17:20, NIV). As believers, there are almost certainly going to be times when we feel that our lives, identities, and geographical locations fail to match up to the splendor of the God whom we worship and believe in. During such times we must remind ourselves that:

> *Our current circumstances are not the final determinant of where we will finish.*

So, despite how rough things may look right now, fully exercise your faith and continually try to discover the divine purpose for which your life was designed. For He molds us as potters mold their clay. As God said to Jeremiah,

> "Go down to the potter's shop, and I will speak to you there." So I did as he told me and found the potter working at his wheel. But the jar he was making did not turn out as he had hoped, so he crushed it into a lump of clay again and started over. Then the LORD gave me this message: "O Israel, can I not do to you as this potter has done to his clay? As the clay is in the potter's hand, so are you in my hand (Jeremiah 18:2–6, NLT).

But who are you, a human being, to talk back to God? "Shall what is formed say to the one who formed it, 'Why did you make me like this?'" Does not the potter have the right to make out of the same lump of clay some pottery for special purposes and some for common use? (Romans 9:20–21, NIV).

Jochebed had no way of knowing that, out of every pregnant mother in Goshen, she alone would be granted the miracle of seeing her son saved. But there was more: Moses would grow up to become a mighty leader, not only defeating Pharaoh and his powerful military but also being selected by God to receive the laws that govern the entire Judeo-Christian world.

Moses was held in the highest regard by the Egyptians and was considered "a very great man in the land of Egypt, respected by Pharaoh's officials and the Egyptian people alike" (Exodus 11:3, NLT).

Since then, no prophet has risen in Israel like Moses, whom the LORD knew face to face (Deuteronomy 34:10, NIV).

For the law was given through Moses (John 1:17, NIV).

Thus the woman whose name in Hebrew means "God's glory" defeated Pharaoh through faith.

Ironically enough, her son was to grow up in Pharaoh's own household. How comforting this must have been for Jochebed! Just imagine her pleasure every time that her enemy's daughter paid her. I like to think that she did a little faith dance every time the payment arrived! As some people might say today *"Sweet!"*

In terms of your own faith journeys, please remember that although you might not have all the answers quite yet, God will guide you through the dark valleys and safely through to the other side.

> The Lord is my shepherd, I lack nothing. He makes me lie down in green pastures, he leads me beside quiet waters, He refreshes my soul. He guides me along the right paths for his name's sake. Even though I walk through the darkest valley, I will fear no evil, for you are with me; your rod and your staff, they comfort me" (Psalm 23:1–4, NIV).

In short, God accomplishes His plans through ordinary human beings. When he chose to reveal His glory through Jochebed, a great deliverer was born. God does things in His own way and in His own time. Alleluia! "He has made everything beautiful in its time. He has also set eternity in the human heart; yet no one can fathom what God has done from beginning to end" (Ecclesiastes 3:11, NIV).

So remember, even if God appears to be ignoring your cries for help or appears to be delaying His answer, He might be working on a far greater miracle than the one you're asking for!

Do you believe and receive this?

Chapter Three

His Mighty Hands at Work

*Rise from the dust, O Jerusalem. Sit in a place
of honor. Remove the chains of slavery from
your neck, O captive daughter of Zion.*

—Isaiah 52:2 (NLT)

We have arrived at one of my favorite lessons to be drawn from Jochebed's own life, which is this:

Don't compare your life to anyone else's!

You may be wondering how this might be relevant.

Well, at the time when Jochebed's baby was born, already hundreds—if not thousands—of Hebrew newborns had been slaughtered. (We'll probably never know how many.) If Jochebed had begun to play the game of comparisons and guilt-tripped over all the lives that had already been lost, instead of focusing on saving her own child, she probably would have been paralyzed into inaction. She might have thought along these lines:

Why should my son be the only one to survive this cruel law? The forces ranged against us are too strong to fight!

Don't these other families and babies deserve a miracle too? Why should we be the only ones to be spared?

These and possibly many other similarly guilt-laden thoughts could well have occupied Jochebed's mind, and the opportunity been lost. These kinds of faith-destroying tactics—so often employed by our enemies—will slow down our faith momentum and hinder us from receiving those good things that God has in store for us. And although such questions would have been extremely reasonable for anyone in Jochebed's position to ask, when it comes to making faith decisions, we're only responsible for ourselves. There are no "one size fits all" answers when it comes to receiving anything from God. Each person is created by God with a unique destiny. No two lives are exactly the same; even identical twins have different fingerprints and unique destinies, given to them by God. "For we are God's masterpiece. He has created us anew in Christ Jesus, so we can do the good things he planned for us long ago" (Ephesians 2:10, NLT).

No matter how similar your life may appear to be to someone else's—or how close you might feel to that person—each individual is a unique masterpiece, created by God and possessing an individual destiny. It's possible for people to share identical looks, talents, even likes and dislikes, yet each has been given a specific assignment by God. In other words, even though members of our own families or communities might have fallen victim to adverse circumstances, it doesn't mean that we'll all also end up in the same place! This is because our Creator has equipped each person with special gifts and attributes that perfectly fit the unique destiny that He has in mind for us.

> *Never attempt to live someone else's life, or attempt*
> *to make their outcomes your own. Instead, seek*
> *God for His answer to your own needs.*

Now this might, at first glance, seem a pretty selfish way of looking at things, but on closer examination, is this unfair? Had Jochebed failed to take advantage of the opportunity to rescue her son, Moses would almost certainly have died. However, from reading the Scriptures, as well as with the benefit of hindsight, we know that Moses was always intended to be the miracle that God sent to the Hebrews. Moses couldn't be allowed to die—not only for his own sake but for the sake of his entire nation!

Only the unique plan that God has for each person will be the perfect fit for that person's life. Guilt-tripping or comparing oneself to others isn't useful. Instead, we must discover and attempt to deliver God's carefully designed plans for our lives. This isn't a selfish mindset; it's a healthy one. Our destinies are uniquely crafted for us by God. Whom can we trust, if not Him?

Our lives will only work out for us in the way that God intends when we have faith in His vision and seek answers from Him, not from our own instincts. Moses' mother would not merely have cost her son his life had she played the comparison game with other Goshen families, she would also have sabotaged her own nation's best chance at rescue. Her people would have remained slaves in Egypt—at least until God could raise up another deliverer.

Comparison games (and guilt) are both perennial enemies of faith. We need to be alert to these deadly weapons in the enemy's hands. Jochebed clearly understood this, as she seized this opportunity to rescue, not only her son but the Israelites too. Any other decision would have meant death to an entire people.

But—thanks be to God!—this woman of faith did not fail in her God-assigned role. Her son did indeed survive to help the Hebrews escape from Egypt and triumph over their enemies. All as a direct result of his family's trust in God. The question of whether we should also pursue God's path for us or submit to the same fate as others will probably be presented to most of us at some point in our lives.

*Surrendering to negative circumstances is not
the best way to tackle unpleasant interruptions
or unwelcome challenges in our lives.*

God is primarily responsible for fulfilling His plans and purposes, but we need to trust and obey Him—as Jochebed did—so that matters can work out as He has planned.

The right approach to any problem is to seek God's will first, and then take faith-filled, wise, and decisive action to overcome whatever the issues may be. We might end up helping a lot more people than we ever imagined—Jochebed and her family certainly did!

Although Moses' mother was almost certainly experiencing a high level of guilt for successfully hiding her own son while others' babies were murdered, she didn't allow such feelings to prevent her from rescuing her son and, by extension, her nation. Through her faith and obedience, she allowed her son to become the vehicle through which God fulfilled His extraordinary plans. In other words, age, gender, nationality, past history . . . none of these disqualify anyone from receiving God's help. Having unshakeable faith is *all* that we need. Also, no worry is too big or too small for our loving Creator to solve!

We are the only ones who can prevent the fulfillment of God's plans for our lives--by responding to Him with doubt or disbelief.

Every blessing will be ours, if we simply have faith enough to place our trust in God.

Before signing off on this part of our discussion, it would be wrong not to address the faith of the mothers whose babies were killed by the Egyptians while Moses was safe in his mother's arms. We can all certainly empathize with any feelings of resentment, even rage, that they may have harbored toward Jochebed if they even suspected that she might have saved her son while their own sons had been murdered.

Attempting to comfort grieving parents with platitudes would not have gone down well. It would have been extremely difficult to convince these grieving parents that God had loved their children as much as He loved Jochebed's. These feelings are so understandable—yet God was still hard at work in their own lives too, because Moses' birth signaled the end of the Hebrew's captivity in Egypt. Even though they could probably never have imagined it, every single Hebrew slave needed this particular baby to survive. Moses' victory would ultimately be their victory too.

This is another reason why we should resist comparing our lives to others' but instead should continue to trust in God. Regardless of how unfair things might seem to us, we'll rarely possess the full story or entirely understand all that God is doing on our behalf. Yes, it would be hard to expect these poor bereaved mothers not to harbor hatred toward Moses and his family—they can be forgiven for feeling resentful—but, especially when in distress, it's best not to try to figure out God. Instead, just rely on Him for the grace to pull through.

Just one person's "Yes!" to God can have an impact on the lives of huge numbers of people. Although the people of Goshen lost so many of their children, God was still fully and constantly at work on the Hebrews' behalf. He goes so far as to assure us—in His word—that there is eternal reward for those who suffer great losses while fighting to receive their ultimate triumphs.

> People died still believing what God had promised them. "They did not receive what was promised, but they saw it all from a distance and welcomed it. They agreed that they were foreigners and nomads here on earth" (Hebrews 11:13, NLT).

> "All these people earned a good reputation because of their faith, yet none of them received all that God had promised. For God had something better in mind for us, so that they would not reach perfection without us" (Hebrews 11:39–40, NLT).

> "For our present troubles are small and won't last very long. Yet they produce for us a glory that vastly outweighs them and will last forever!

So we don't look at the troubles we can see now; rather, we fix our gaze on things that cannot be seen. For the things we see now will soon be gone, but the things we cannot see will last forever" (2 Corinthians 4:17–18, NLT; see also Lamentations 3).

Of course, many others in the Bible also pressed through grave dangers in order to receive God's highest blessings. God works through even our most terrible experiences to produce good results in our lives, and in the lives of others. This might seem a rather bitter pill to swallow, but I implore you to continue to trust Him, even though you might be enduring tremendous pain.

Although you might never have volunteered for God's "mission impossible," I would hope that you yield to His will, remembering that His highest rewards are reserved for those who place utter trust in Him. After all, we are assured, again and again, that God is working out a far better eternal outcome than we could even imagine!

We'll be learning more about this challenging aspect of having unshakeable faith later on. Meanwhile:

Never give up your hope in God. Remember that His priority is to change us—not just our circumstances.

As already mentioned, what may feel excruciating may still work for our eternal good. Jesus Himself didn't wish to endure all that He had to, including death on a cross. But for the sake of humankind, He yielded Himself to God's eternal plan of salvation and paid for all our sins. "He walked away, about a stone's throw, and knelt down and prayed, 'Father, if you are willing, please take this cup of suffering away from me. Yet I want your will to be done, not mine'" (Luke 22:41–42, NLT).

Although many people, myself included, would never volunteer for any of God's "missions impossible," difficult and painful processes are sometimes required in order to bring about His purpose to the earth. It's particularly difficult to exercise faith in God while enduring severe trials. But, although we may not even recognize it, God is constantly at work in our lives. He may sometimes move in mysterious ways, but this doesn't mean that we ought to allow fear and doubt to reign in our hearts instead of God's word.

As an example: from the moment that Jochebed's baby was born, the Hebrew people's longed-for deliverer had finally come. Yet, crushed by their brutal captivity, they couldn't recognize God's gift. Similarly, we may not always recognize God's responses to our own needs—even though they may be right in front of us! Despite this, He is ceaselessly working on our behalf. God loves every single one of us. Everything that He does springs from His love, "because God is love" (1 John 4:8, NIV). And "love does not delight in evil" (1 Corinthians 13:6, NIV).

I hope that the following quote from renowned preacher Charles Spurgeon will also be of comfort.

*God is too good to be unkind and He is too
wise to be mistaken. And when we cannot
trace His hand, we must trust His heart.*

Although things may not always work out exactly the way that we want, remember that God's purpose is higher. He's working things out for your temporal and your eternal good. He may choose what looks to us like a harder, slower, and much more complex way to resolve our problems. When you don't understand God's ways, trust His heart and rest on the true security of His promises. Because they're true!

"Oh, the depth of the riches of the wisdom and knowledge of God! How unsearchable his judgments, and his paths beyond tracing out!" (Romans 11:33, NIV). Someday we will be blessed with entire understanding. Then we'll find out that God was walking alongside us during our every trial, and that His mighty hands were always at work on our behalf. He was probably carrying us when we couldn't walk!

When troubles of any kind come your way, consider it an opportunity for great joy. For you know that when your faith is tested, your endurance has a chance to grow. So let it grow, for when your endurance is fully developed, you will be perfect and complete, needing nothing. If you need wisdom, ask our generous God and he will give it to you. He will not rebuke you for asking. But when you ask him, be sure that your faith is in God alone. Do not waver, for a person with divided loyalty is as unsettled as a wave of the sea that is blown and tossed by the wind. Such people should not expect to receive anything from the Lord. Their loyalty is divided between God and the world, and they are unstable in everything they do (James 1:2–8, NLT).

Moses' story reveals that God can perform extraordinary feats, using ordinary people and handwoven baskets. Like Jochebed, sometimes all we can do is to mitigate negative circumstances and wait patiently for God. "Just as you cannot understand the path of the wind or the mystery of a tiny baby growing in its mother's womb, so you cannot understand the activity of God, who does all things" (Ecclesiastes 11:5, NLT).

People who choose to believe in God and His promises
are never really powerless or without hope.

When we make the decision to be unshakeable in our faith, we position ourselves to receive God's highest blessings. The unique sets of talents that we each possess have been given to us by God and will come into play when we answer His call. In fact, if you are currently facing severe difficulties, you may be in the process of being recruited for far higher blessings than you could have dreamed of—or volunteered for!

Unquantifiable blessings will be ours once our painful ordeals are over. So in order to fulfill the destiny and the plans that God has uniquely designed for you, accept God's will for you with all your soul and all your heart. In other words, seek His plan for your life, not somebody else's! Summon up the courage to manifest triumph over the circumstances of your own life, whatever they might be.

> "Arise, shine, for your light has come, and the glory of the LORD rises upon you. See, darkness covers the earth and thick darkness is over the peoples, but the LORD rises upon you and his glory appears over you" (Isaiah 60:1–2, NIV).

The smallest measure of faith, when fully exercised, can prove both powerful and significant. Be strong enough to demonstrate wisdom and courage, ensuring that your actions are fully rooted in your faith. Believe that God is moving on your behalf. And always remember that patience, as well as faith, is required to receive the full manifestation of God's promises. So "imitate those who through faith and patience inherit what has been promised" (Hebrews 6:12, NIV).

"Who knows whether you have not come to the kingdom for such a time as this?" (Esther 4:14, ESV).

God in the end did utterly obliterate Pharaoh and his mighty army. But not before giving him many opportunities to repent—something Pharaoh stubbornly and repeatedly refused to do.

"Do not say, 'I will avenge this evil!' Wait on the LORD, and He will rescue you" (Proverbs 20:22, Berean Study Bible).

*What actions can you take now—this
moment—to begin to mitigate your
own negative circumstances?*

Chapter Four

A FAMILY OF CHAMPIONS

Those who trust in the LORD are like
Mount Zion, which cannot be shaken.

—PSALM 125:1 (NIV)

One of the first miracles Moses received was being blessed with a mother willing to fight for his life. By exercising her faith, one day at a time, until receiving her miracle, Moses' mother gave us a glimpse into the inner workings of genuine biblical faith. Her faith in God was emphatically rewarded when her son was rescued by the Egyptian princess—and later when God granted the Israelites a massive victory over their oppressors.

So as things turned out, his being a boy was God's perfect plan for Moses. Jochebed's baby would not have been better off being born a girl: a boy was the ideal gender for God's intentions. It bears repeating that God created every single one of us for a specific purpose, and that we each possess a unique destiny. Spending time in His presence will help us to discover exactly who we are and exactly what we have been created by God to do.

*Fulfilling God's purpose for us will bring
us the most contentment and peace.*

Have you also given any thought to the fact that, even though babies are always considered perfect and adorable by their parents, if there ever was a baby whose life depended on his being super-cute that baby was Moses? God had created such an extraordinary baby for Jochedbed that "when she saw that he was [especially] beautiful" she couldn't bear the thought of parting from him, (Exodus 2:2, AMP).

Just one look at that face was all that it took to give his mother the supernatural love, strength, and courage to do battle with the most powerful ruler of the time. Moses' appearance was uniquely designed by God to fill his mother's heart with determination, passion, and fearlessness. She would spare no effort to keep her newborn alive.

*Passion gives us courage, and great passion
can produce great courage. It takes courage as
well as faith to accomplish great things.*

Moses' appearance, as well as his cries, must equally have tugged at the heartstrings of the Egyptian princess.

Bonding instantly with someone else's baby—possibly also moved by pity for the Hebrews—she too became willing to stand courageously as his guardian, defying *her own father's* cruel law. (Have you ever wondered what would have become of the princess had Pharaoh found out that she had not only defied him but had paid a slave to defy him too?)

In short, taking Moses into her family was not only a risky but also an extremely brave act. It seems that everyone who beheld baby Moses was moved by God to do whatever was necessary in order to protect him! It is also interesting to reflect that Jochebed and her family may have been slaves, but they had never allowed their *minds* to become enslaved. (I suspect that we can all empathize. Had I been a Hebrew mother during this terrible period, nothing less than Pharaoh's death could have assuaged my fury. Murdering babies is, frankly, about as low as you can go. And although God could have prevented this particular ruler from ascending the throne or even removed him from power, He chose not to.)

*Submitting to God when we have no idea
what He is doing can feel unbearably tough. It
requires the highest level of trust and faith.*

Another lesson we can learn from Jochebed is how to raise fearless and faith-filled children in the teeth of adverse circumstances. Despite enduring the unimaginable sufferings of slavery, this courageous couple raised their children to be leaders, not followers. Young Miriam was a warrior, just like her mother. She displayed intelligence and boldness beyond her years when the Egyptian princess discovered her brother on the river. Miriam had the audacity to ask a princess if she could assist in locating a wet nurse for a baby who was not, legally, even allowed to be alive. Then she rushed home and triumphantly returned with her own mother!

I don't know about you, but—had I been in Miriam's shoes on that day—I'd have rushed home, quietly freaking out, and repeating under my breath, "My brother is safe! My brother is safe! An Egyptian princess took him from the river!" Because Miriam ran so fast that she was probably gasping for breath, it might have taken her mother a minute or two to figure out what she was saying. Plus, she would not have wanted their neighbors to find out what was going on.

It took nerve as well as brilliance for this young child to come up with such an ingenious plan under such pressure. Truly, Miriam was awe-inspiring—someone raised by an amazing mother to receive the blessings of strong faith. How else could a child of that age have come up with such a creative response under enemy fire? Jochebed's daughter not only negotiated the deal of a lifetime with the princess, she enabled her own mother to defy Pharaoh's law and Pharaoh's power.

Miriam was old enough to know that placing Moses on the river was an absolute last-ditch effort to save his life. Most children in her position would not have had enough nerve to stay anywhere near that basket. Most would have prayed for their baby brother from a safe distance, not wishing to witness any calamity that might befall. I also strongly doubt that most children would have had enough determination to approach the princess, knowing how bitterly the Pharaoh despised and hated the Hebrews. But after keeping watch over her brother, Miriam took every chance to demonstrate her own fearless faith.

You'll have heard the idiom, "To have some nerve," used to describe someone both audacious and fearless. I've coined a new phrase to describe what this brave young girl did: "To have some faith nerve!" Miriam's cool-headedness under these scary circumstances surely took "faith nerve" on her part. Her entire family demonstrated unshakeable faith in God, risking death to defy Pharaoh's law. They never once let their fears defeat them.

Jochebed's family teaches us to hold on to unflinching faith, even when in the grip of our fiercest enemies.

This family had no civil rights, no financial assets, and probably nothing of monetary value in this world, but they still managed to pull off a spectacular victory against the cruelest ruler of their times—by placing their utmost trust in God.

After having been believed to be the son of the Egyptian princess for many years, Moses grew to adulthood, overcame several difficult challenges, and finally took up his God-given assignment to lead the Hebrew people out of Egypt. Moses had been allowed to survive, in order to reveal God's mighty power. Our heavenly father is mighty to save, and nothing can stop the work of His powerful hands.

> The LORD your God is with you, the Mighty Warrior who saves (Zephaniah 3:17, NIV).

> Then the LORD said to Moses, "Go to Pharaoh and say to him, 'this is what the LORD says: Let my people go, so that they may worship me" (Exodus 8:1, NIV).

Here is another observation: God certainly had the power to make every pregnant woman in Goshen give birth only to girls, but this course would have fulfilled Pharaoh's desire and eventually wiped out the Israelites. We may sometimes long to have our immediate troubles resolved with some massive display of God's power, but God has no need to prove His power, to us or to anyone. He's already done that, through His creation! "For ever since the world was created, people have seen the earth and sky. Through everything God made, they can clearly see his invisible qualities—his eternal power and divine nature. So they have no excuse for not knowing God" (Romans 1:20, NLT).

God determines the best course of action to release us from our troubles. All-patient and all-knowing, He is not confined to any single way of answering our prayers. He can work through natural or supernatural means for our temporal and eternal good. Our own families may be in urgent need of divine rescue, but if He appears to be delaying His answers to our prayers—or even saying "No"—remember that this might be a precursor to a far greater "Yes" from Him. "For there is nothing that God cannot do" (Luke 1:37, GNT).

Our health, relationships, businesses, finances, etc., may at different times seem in urgent need of divine intervention. When this happens, choose to place your trust in God. Our loving, heavenly Father is infinitely wise. He will determine what is best for us. I fully recognize that it can be quite difficult to hold on to faith during challenging times. But I implore you to hold tightly to both faith and hope. The following promises from God can be of some reassurance:

"I am the LORD, the God of all the peoples of the world. Is anything too hard for me?" (Jeremiah 32:27, NLT).

Since ancient times no one has heard, no ear has perceived, no eye has seen any God besides

you, who acts on behalf of those who wait for
him (Isaiah 64:4, NIV).

Allow Jochebed and her family's example to help
you to dig deeply and to exercise your own unshakeable
faith in God. Be faithful in whatever God has currently
entrusted to you. For He promises, "A crown of beauty
for ashes, a joyous blessing instead of mourning, festive
praise instead of despair. In their righteousness, they will
be like great oaks that the LORD has planted for his
own glory" (Isaiah 61:3, NLT).

So press on, with God's help. All three of Jochebed's
children grew to become great leaders in Israel. Moses'
older brother Aaron was first in the priestly line established by God, while his brave sister Miriam became a
prophetess and leader over the nation. They were not
a perfect family, but they served a perfect God. (See
Exodus 28:1 and 40–41, NIV.)

> "For I brought you out of Egypt and redeemed
> you from slavery. I sent Moses, Aaron, and
> Miriam to help you" (Micah 6:4, NLT). (See
> also Exodus 15:20.)

> "I tell you, you can pray for anything, and if you
> believe that you've received it, it will be yours"
> (Mark 11:24, NLT).

Where you begin in life is no indicator of where you will end up. Never allow your current circumstances to define you. Instead allow the word of God to shape your thinking.

Have faith in God (Mark 11:22, NIV).

And without faith it is impossible to please God (Hebrews 11:6, NIV).

The choices that we make build our character and inform our faith. Making the decision to exercise our faith, especially when hard-pressed, brings God's highest blessings into our lives. First, release your situation to Him. Things may not always go exactly the way that we most wish for, but if we choose to trust God, the outcomes will bring Him glory. Our all-seeing, all-knowing, and all-powerful Creator knows exactly what He is doing! My prayer for us all is that we will take heart and place our trust in Him.

"Be still, and know that I am God! I will be honored by every nation. I will be honored throughout the world" (Psalm 46:10, NLT). If we answer our own unique calling from Him—as Jochebed's family did—then God will work through our every problem and produce awesome results in our lives. Moses' mother held tightly to her faith and God's much bigger plan was fulfilled. Moses' story has since been made into blockbuster movies, musicals, and award-winning dramas. His life continues to inspire today, and will for generations to come. His survival was a pure impossibility by human standards, but, "With God all things are possible" (Matthew 19:26, NIV).

So what additional lessons can we take from all these?

Resist evil in every form, and draw comfort, wisdom, and strength from Jochebed's example of faith. Pray for grace from God in order to triumph over your own difficulties. It is possible to raise an amazing family, even under the most difficult circumstances. Even the most insignificant-looking lives can hold seeds of greatness. Fight the good fight in order to experience God's victory in your own life. And, most of all, never give up. Moses was not created to die as a newborn baby, but instead to be his nation's deliverer. (I was tempted to title this section "No Longer Slaves!").

> Be strong in the Lord and in his mighty power. Put on the full armor of God, so that you can take your stand against the devil's schemes. For our struggle is not against flesh and blood, but against the rulers, against the authorities, against the powers of this dark world and against the spiritual forces of evil in the heavenly realms. Therefore put on the full armor of God, so that when the day of evil comes, you may be able to stand your ground, and after you have done

everything, to stand. Stand firm then, with the belt of truth buckled around your waist, with the breastplate of righteousness in place, and with your feet fitted with the readiness that comes from the gospel of peace. In addition to all this, take up the shield of faith, with which you can extinguish all the flaming arrows of the evil one. Take the helmet of salvation and the sword of the Spirit, which is the word of God (Ephesians 6:10–17, NIV).

It takes courage as well as faith to exercise unshakeable faith in God. If Jochebed and her family managed it, do you believe that you can, too?

Chapter Five

RECEIVING AND GROWING
STRONGER IN YOUR FAITH

*So faith comes from hearing that is,
hearing the Good News about Christ.*

—ROMANS 10:17 (NLT)

I f there is any "catch" to faith, it's that faith is so simple. "Truly I tell you, anyone who will not receive the kingdom of God like a little child will never enter it" (Mark 10:15, NIV).

Faith requires us to exercise a childlike trust in God. The process by which faith comes begins with hearing God's word, believing it, and then taking decisive action based on what God has quickened us to hear. The actions that we take demonstrate the conviction of our hearts, the *faith* in our hearts.

In the same way, faith by itself, if it is not accompanied by action, is dead. But someone will say, "You have faith; I have deeds." Show me your faith without deeds, and I will show you my faith by my deeds (James 2:17–18, NIV).

Can't you see that faith without good deeds is useless? (James 2:20, NLT).

You can identify them by their fruit, that is, by the way they act. Can you pick grapes from thornbushes, or figs from thistles?" (Matthew 7:16, NLT).

Genuine biblical faith can be described as *the conviction that comes from hearing, believing, and receiving God's word, the conviction that causes our hearts to settle on a clear course of action.*

When we hear God's word through the Scriptures, allowing them to ignite divinely guaranteed expectations in our hearts, this inspires hope. And hope paves the way for conviction and belief; true faith will follow.

Now faith is the assurance (title deed, confirmation) of things hoped for (divinely guaranteed), and the evidence of things not seen [the conviction of their reality—faith comprehends as fact what cannot be experienced by the physical senses] (Hebrews 11:1, AMP).

Merriam-Webster's secular definition of hope is, "A desire with anticipation: to want something to happen or be true." But divinely guaranteed expectation or biblical hope is special—and different. It originates from God, through His word, not from human desire. God is the guarantor of His every promise. He is the only one with infinite power, the power to bring all that He has spoken of to pass.

> For when he spoke, the world began! It appeared at his command (Psalm 33:9, NLT).

> By faith we understand that the entire universe was formed at God's command, that what we now see did not come from anything that can be seen (Hebrews 11:3, NLT).

> Let every created thing give praise to the LORD, for he issued his command, and they came into being (Psalm 148:5, NLT).

A life of genuine faith begins when human beings allow the good news of God's word to ignite hope in their hearts, and when they become convinced that what He has said is true. Their faith in God serves as proof that what they believe will be made manifest. However, a life of faith cannot begin until we restore our broken relationship with God. "It's your sins that have cut you off from God" (Isaiah 59:2, NLT). The scriptures inform us that all human beings are born with original sin and that our sinful nature was inherited from the first two human beings, our original "parents," Adam and Eve. "For everyone has sinned; we all fall short of God's glorious standard" (Romans 3:23, NLT).

God had entrusted Adam and Eve with full authority over the planet that He had created for them and given to them. These two received more blessings than anyone could either ask for or imagine, yet still they chose to rebel against God. They committed the ultimate act of treason, bringing destruction upon all of creation. (See Genesis 1–3.)

The sinful nature that humans inherited from Adam and Eve predisposes us to a life of rebellion against God, because sin separates us from Him. The evil consequences of the original rebellion brought near-total destruction on all of creation; great suffering and all manner of evil and death came to our planet.

Things would have continued in this way forever had our loving Creator not chosen to forgive us our sins and to offer us a free and complete pardon. He did this by sacrificing Jesus, His only begotten son, on the cross to pay for all of humankind's past, present, and future sins. In other words, when a person hears the message of God's salvation and believes it, that soul receives a free pardon from God. This restores the broken communion with Him.

For the wages of sin is death, but the free gift of God is eternal life through Christ Jesus our Lord (Romans 6:23, NLT).

For God loved the world so much that he gave his only Son, so that everyone who believes in him may not die but have eternal life (John 3:16, GNT).

So now there is no condemnation for those who belong to Christ Jesus. And because you belong to him, the power of the life-giving Spirit has freed you from the power of sin that leads to death (Romans 8:1–2, NLT).

It is the *grace* of God that makes it possible for every single human to be accepted back into His eternal family and to begin a life of faith. However, there is *no other way.* The *only* way to begin a life of authentic faith is to accept the forgiveness offered to all humankind by God through Jesus' death for us on the cross.

Jesus answered, "I am the way and the truth and the life. No one comes to the Father except through me" (John 14:6, NIV).

Jesus is "the stone you builders rejected, which has become the cornerstone." Salvation is found

in no one else, for there is no other name under
heaven given to mankind by which we must be
saved (Acts 4:11–12, NIV).

After we receive the free and loving gift of salvation,
God's Holy Spirit can begin the work of transforming us
into God's loving nature instead of our old, sinful, rebel-
lious selves.

God's love has been poured out into our hearts
through the Holy Spirit, who has been given to
us (Romans 5:5, NIV).

For all who are led by the Spirit of God are
children of God. So you have not received a
spirit that makes you fearful slaves. Instead,
you received God's Spirit when he adopted you
as his own children. Now we call him, Abba,
Father. For his Spirit joins with our spirit to
affirm that we are God's children (Romans
8:14–16, NLT). (Note: "Abba" is an intimate,
almost childlike, term for a father.)

God is the source of our lives and of every blessing
that we enjoy. Jesus completely obliterated the evil consequences of our sins so that anyone, regardless of their past
sins, their ethnicity, their gender, or their socio-economic
status, could receive God's forgiveness and enjoy the life

that they were originally meant to live, the life of abundance God wants for each one of us. But these blessings can only begin with hearing and believing the message of Christ, which is faith. And it's only after establishing our right relationship with God that we can begin to grow in faith. When our desires become aligned with God's—when they no longer spring from our old sinful ways—God delights in fulfilling them. "Take delight in the LORD, and he will give you the desires of your heart (Psalm 37:4, NIV).

God has also promised in the Scriptures that He will guide us and illuminate our paths when we have faith enough to enter into a new relationship with Him. "Your word is a lamp for my feet, a light on my path (Psalm 119:105, NIV).

We need to constantly remember that, even though God's free gift of salvation cost human beings nothing, it cost God everything. Redeemed human beings—blessed with God's enabling power and grace—owe Him their gratitude and love in return.

> May you be filled with joy, always thanking the father. He has enabled you to share in the inheritance that belongs to his people, who live in the light. For he has rescued us from the kingdom of darkness and transferred us into the Kingdom of his dear Son (Colossians 1:11–13, NLT).

Before the physical death of Jesus Christ, humans were saved on the basis of His atoning sacrifice yet to come. All that was required was to believe in, and to be obedient to, the revelation of God that they had been allowed to hear up to that point. But since Jesus was revealed in human form, salvation can only be attained *by placing our faith in His atoning sacrifice for sin.* After that, we can deepen our connection with God by continuing to seek Him, and by abiding in Him.

"If you abide in me, and my words abide in you, ask whatever you wish, and it will be done for you!" (John 15:7, NLT). Access to God's help is also divinely guaranteed by His word. We have so much to be thankful to God for!

> So let us come boldly to the throne of our gracious God. There we will receive his mercy, and we will find grace to help us when we need it most (Hebrews 4:16, NLT).

> For everyone born of God overcomes the world. This is the victory that has overcome the world, even our faith. Who is it that overcomes the world? Only the one who believes that Jesus is the Son of God (1 John 5:4–5, NIV).

You may be thinking that entering into a relationship with God can't be quite so simple. Many people believe that the way of salvation must be a lot tougher, or at least more complicated. Can anyone, from anywhere, truly just hear, believe in, and receive God's free pardon simply through accepting that the price for all human sins—past, present, and future—has been paid for them by Jesus? (There's *got* to be a catch, right?) People wonder: Shouldn't there be more that humans have to do? Shouldn't they have experienced at least one miraculous sign from God before being expected to have unshakeable faith in Him?

Digging further into the Scriptures will help us to answer these and other questions. We need to better understand the role of Christ's sacrifice in order to absorb how faith comes to human beings. Because despite God's best efforts—given the way we're made—not even His most spectacular acts may be enough.

Very early on Sunday morning the women went to the tomb, taking the spices they had prepared. They found that the stone had been rolled away from the entrance. So they went in, but they didn't find the body of the Lord Jesus. As they stood there puzzled, two men suddenly appeared to them, clothed in dazzling robes. The women were terrified and bowed with their faces to the ground. Then the men asked, "Why are you looking among the dead for someone who is alive? He isn't here! He is risen from the dead! Remember what he told you back in Galilee, that the Son of Man must be betrayed into the hands of sinful men and be crucified, and that

he would rise again on the third day." Then they remembered that he had said this. So they rushed back from the
tomb to tell his eleven disciples and everyone else what
had happened. It was Mary Magdalene, Joanna, Mary
the mother of James, and several other women who told
the apostles what had happened. But the story sounded
like nonsense to the men, so, *they didn't believe it* (Luke
24:1–11, NLT [emphasis added]).

> Then the two from Emmaus told their story of
> how Jesus had appeared to them as they were
> walking along the road, and how they had rec-
> ognized him as he was breaking the bread. And
> just as they were telling about it, Jesus him-
> self was suddenly standing there among them.
> "Peace be with you," he said. But the whole
> group was startled and frightened, thinking
> they were seeing a ghost! "Why are you fright-
> ened?" he asked. *"Why are your hearts filled with
> doubt?* [Emphasis added.]
>
> "Look at my hands. Look at my feet. You
> can see that it's really me. Touch me and make
> sure that I am not a ghost, because ghosts don't
> have bodies, as you see that I do." As he spoke,
> he showed them his hands and his feet. Still
> they stood there in disbelief, filled with joy and
> wonder.

Then he asked them, "Do you have anything here to eat?" They gave him a piece of broiled fish, and he ate it as they watched. Then he said, "When I was with you before, I told you that everything written about me in the Law of Moses and the prophets and in the Psalms must be fulfilled." Then he opened their minds to understand the Scriptures. And he said, "Yes, it was written long ago that the Messiah would suffer and die and rise from the dead on the third day. It was also written that this message would be proclaimed in the authority of his name to all the nations, beginning in Jerusalem: 'There is forgiveness of sins for all who repent.' You are witnesses of all these things (Luke 24:35–48, NLT).

In other words, despite personally witnessing perhaps the most spectacular act ever—and despite the evidence of their own eyes *that the resurrected Jesus was standing in their midst*—Jesus' own disciples still found it very hard to have faith.

The greatest miracle has to be the raising of the dead. To this day, technological and other scientific advances have yet to discover death's remedy. Yet even though they had witnessed Jesus perform numberless miracles, including Jesus' having Himself raised the dead (see Luke 8:40–56, 7:11–17; John 11:17–44). Not even

His own disciples were able to accept the truth until they heard the Scriptures themselves from Jesus. His resurrection was met with near-total disbelief until He calmly reminded His disciples of all that God had promised beforehand. Which in turn reminds us that

> *It's only when God's Word is mixed with faith in our hearts that true faith is born. Spectacular and miraculous acts alone are not enough!*

The birth, death, and resurrection of Jesus had been prophesied for hundreds of years, and had finally been fulfilled in plain sight. But when people choose not to believe or fail to act on the miracles revealed to them, it will do them no good at all.

> For we have heard the Good News, just as they did. They heard the message, but it did them no good, because when they heard it, they did not accept it with faith (Hebrews 4:2, GNT).

> God does perform miracles and awesome wonders, but the Scriptures teach us to "walk by faith, not by sight" (2 Corinthians 5:7, ESV).

"Well," you may be thinking, "Jochebed and many others in the Bible might well have had stronger personalities than I, no wonder they possess stronger faith!" But faith has nothing to do with the strength of our personalities or even with personal willpower. Instead, authentic biblical faith is based *solely* on how much of God's word we allow into our hearts.

> Above all else, guard your heart, for everything you do flows from it (Proverbs 4:23, NIV).

> For as he thinks within himself, so he is (Proverbs 23:7, ISV).

When I was a brand-new believer, I used to pray that God would allow me to have some undisputable spiritual experience, in order to strengthen my new and fragile faith. I used to think, "Perhaps if I could have a vision, or a visit from one of His angelic messengers, I'd be more fervently convinced of God's existence and believe still more strongly in His word." Have you ever wondered what might help you believe more strongly in God? If so, then I hope that this excerpt will provide assurance that faith comes from simply hearing, accepting, and believing God's message.

> There was a rich man who was dressed in purple and fine linen and lived in luxury every day. At his gate was laid a beggar named Lazarus,

covered with sores and longing to eat what fell from the rich man's table. Even the dogs came and licked his sores.

The time came when the beggar died and the angels carried him to Abraham's side. The rich man also died and was buried. In Hades, where he was in torment, he looked up and saw Abraham far away, with Lazarus by his side. So he called to him, 'Father Abraham, have pity on me and send Lazarus to dip the tip of his finger in water and cool my tongue, because I am in agony in this fire.'

But Abraham replied, 'Son, remember that in your lifetime you received your good things, while Lazarus received bad things, but now he is comforted here and you are in agony. And besides all this, between us and you a great chasm has been set in place, so that those who want to go from here to you cannot, nor can anyone cross over from there to us.'

He answered, 'Then I beg you, father, send Lazarus to my family, for I have five brothers. Let him warn them, so that they will not also come to this place of torment.'

Abraham replied, 'They have Moses and the Prophets; let them listen to them.'

'No, father Abraham,' he said, 'but if someone from the dead goes to them, they will repent.'

He said to him, if they do not listen to Moses and the Prophets, they will not be convinced even if someone rises from the dead (Luke 16:19–31, NIV).

In short, even experiencing miracles may not produce genuine and enduring faith. If we choose *not* to believe in God's word, the fault doesn't lie with God! If we long for all the wonderful, sometimes miraculous, blessings that God wants us to have, we have to accept that they all spring from our personal faith in Him.

> *Experiencing God's supernatural acts can*
> *strengthen our faith, but first we need God's*
> *word to be birthed in our hearts and grow.*

God fulfilled every requirement of righteousness and mercy when He sent His son to die on the cross for our sins. Jesus paid the full penalty for us: He died in our place. Choosing repentance over rebellion and rejecting our sinful ways is how we can truly become God's children—part of His eternal family.

In the beginning the word already existed. The word was with God, and the word was God . . . . So the word became human and made his home among us. He was full of unfailing love and faithfulness (John 1:1, 14, NLT).

To all who believed him and accepted him, he gave the right to become children of God. They are reborn—not with a physical birth resulting from human passion or plan, but a birth that comes from God (John 1:12–13, NLT).

That message is the very message about faith that we preach: If you openly declare that Jesus is Lord and believe in your heart that God raised him from the dead, you will be saved. For it is by believing in your heart that you are made right with God, and it is by openly declaring your faith that you are saved. As the Scriptures tell us, "Anyone who trusts in him will never be disgraced." Jew and Gentile are the same in this respect. They have the same Lord, who gives generously to all who call on him. For "Everyone who calls on the name of the LORD will be saved" (Romans 10:8–13, NLT).

It's up to us. We need to be responsible for our own faith and to keep it strong—by feeding it with the daily nourishment of God's word, and by seeking God's wisdom in everything we do. As mentioned earlier, there's no "one size fits all" answer to our human needs. Each situation that we encounter requires a unique answer from God.

Jesus told him, "People do not live by bread alone, but by every word that comes from the mouth of God" (Matthew 4:4, NLT).

And we also thank God continually because, when you received the word of God, which you heard from us, you accepted it not as a human word, but as it actually is, the word of God, which is indeed at work in you who believe (1 Thessalonians 2:13, NIV).

During both good and bad times, the key to a victorious life is to accept and abide in God's word. This is how faith not only begins but also grows and deepens.

Faith doesn't evolve from magical thinking or from frail human hopes. Instead, as Jochebed's actions proved, it emerges from a childlike trust in God. Then and only then can fallible human beings become partners with God, and become a part of accomplishing His great plans and purposes on earth.

For we are God's fellow workers. You are God's field, God's building (1 Corinthians 3:9, ESV).

Without faith it is impossible to please God, because anyone who comes to him must believe that he exists and that he rewards those who earnestly seek him (Hebrews 11:6, NIV).

If we maintain unshakeable faith in God and allow Him to produce extraordinary results through our lives, our own lives and the lives of people around us will be blessed and God will be pleased. (In other words, "Stay calm, God's got this!")

It's by continually nourishing ourselves with God's word that our faith grows stronger. Are you nourishing yourself daily with His word?

Chapter Six

Staying Vigilant
at All Times

Always keep watch and pray!
—Matthew 26:41 (NLT)

Let's reconnect with Moses in his adult years—fully grown but before he led the Israelites out of Egypt. He was old enough to know that He was not truly the son of the Egyptian princess and had become painfully distressed by his people's sufferings. His biological family still endured extreme brutality at the hand of the Egyptians, and one day Moses decided to take matters into his own hands.

But instead of seeking God for wisdom on how to get justice for his people, Moses reacted emotionally to a disturbing incident and resorted to violence, precipitating a crisis. The action that Moses took changed his life drastically for the worse, but God never gave up on him and eventually led him to his true destiny.

Years later, after Moses had grown up, he went out to his own people and took notice of their heavy burdens. He saw an Egyptian beating up a Hebrew, one of his own people. Looking around and seeing no one else, he killed the Egyptian and hid him in the sand. Going out the next day, Moses noticed two Hebrew men fighting right in front of him. He told the one who was at fault, "Why did you strike your companion?"

The man replied, "Who appointed you to be an official judge over us? Are you planning to kill me like you killed the Egyptian?"

Then Moses became terrified and told himself, "Certainly this event has become known!"

When Pharaoh heard about this matter, he tried to kill Moses. So Moses fled from Pharaoh, settled in the land of Midian, and sat down by a well. Meanwhile, the seven daughters of a certain Midianite priest would come to draw water in order to fill water troughs for their father's sheep. Some shepherds came to drive them away, but Moses got up, came to their rescue, and watered their sheep (Exodus 2:11–17, ISV).

Moses agreed to stay with the man, and he gave his daughter Zipporah to Moses in marriage. Later she gave birth to a son, and Moses named him Gershom because he used to say, "I became an alien in a foreign land." The king of Egypt eventually died, and the Israelis groaned because of the bondage. They cried out, and their cry for deliverance from slavery ascended to God. God heard their groaning and remembered his covenant with Abraham, Isaac, and Jacob. God watched the Israelis and took notice of them (Exodus 2:21–25, ISV).

Now Moses was tending the flock of Jethro his father-in-law, the priest of Midian, and he led the flock to the far side of the wilderness and came to Horeb, the mountain of God. There the angel of the Lord appeared to him in flames of fire from within a bush. Moses saw that though the bush was on fire it did not burn up. So Moses thought, "I will go over and see this strange sight—why the bush does not burn up."

When the Lord saw that he had gone over to look, God called to him from within the bush, "Moses! Moses!"

And Moses said, "Here I am."

"Do not come any closer," God said. "Take off your sandals, for the place where you are standing is holy ground." Then he said, "I am the God of your father, the God of Abraham, the God of Isaac, and the God of Jacob." At this, Moses hid his face, because he was afraid to look at God.

The Lord said, "I have indeed seen the misery of my people in Egypt. I have heard them crying out because of their slave drivers, and I am concerned about their suffering. So I have come down to rescue them from the hand of the Egyptians and to bring them up out of that land into a good and spacious land, a land flowing with milk and honey—the home of the Canaanites, Hittites, Amorites, Perizzites, Hivites, and Jebusites. And now the cry of the Israelites has reached me, and I have seen the way the Egyptians are oppressing them. So now, go. I am sending you to Pharaoh to bring my people the Israelites out of Egypt (Exodus 3:1–10, NIV).

"The elders of Israel will listen to you. Then you and the elders are to go to the king of Egypt and say to him, 'The Lord, the God of the Hebrews, has met with us. Let us take a three-day journey into the wilderness to offer sacrifices to the Lord our God.' But I know that the king of Egypt will not let you go unless a mighty hand compels him. So I will stretch out my hand and strike the Egyptians with all the wonders that I will perform among them. After that, he will let you go.

"And I will make the Egyptians favorably disposed toward this people, so that when you leave you will not go empty-handed. Every woman is to ask her neighbor and any woman living in her house for articles of silver and gold and for clothing, which you will put on your sons and daughters. And so you will plunder the Egyptians" (Exodus 3:18–22, NIV).

Deliverance finally arrived when God sent Moses back to Egypt to deliver His message to Pharaoh—even though, as we know, Pharaoh repeatedly refused to let God's people go. (See Exodus 8:1 and 9:1.) The Egyptians were determined to clutch hold of their massive slave-labor force, while the Israelites continued to suffer.

Meanwhile, Pharaoh's arrogance caused powerful judgments to be unleashed upon Egypt in the form of plagues. First the Nile was turned to blood, then frogs, lice, flies, boils, hail, locusts, and darkness descended, followed by the killing of crucial livestock and, finally, the horrific deaths of every first-born Egyptian child. (Exodus 7:14 and 12:30).

Only after all of these terrible events did the Israelites finally win their struggle to be freed from captivity in Egypt.

During the night Pharaoh summoned Moses and Aaron and said, "Up! Leave my people, you and the Israelites! Go, worship the Lord as you have requested. Take your flocks and herds, as you have said, and go. And also bless me."

The Egyptians urged the people to hurry and leave the country. "For otherwise," they said, "we will all die!" So the people took their dough before the yeast was added, and carried it on their shoulders in kneading troughs wrapped in clothing. The Israelites did as Moses instructed and asked the Egyptians for articles of silver and gold and for clothing. The Lord had made the Egyptians favorably disposed toward the people, and they gave them what they asked for; so they plundered the Egyptians.

The Israelites journeyed from Rameses to Sukkoth. There were about six hundred thousand men on foot, besides women and children. Many other people went up with them, and also large droves of livestock, both flocks and herds (Exodus 12:31–38, NIV).

The Hebrews were asked to leave immediately and Pharaoh even requested their prayers, for himself and for his people. In other words, the Israelites' victory was so overwhelming that the tyrant himself was left humbled and humiliated.

When the Lord restored the fortunes of
   Zion,
We were like those who dreamed.
Our mouths were filled with laughter,
Our tongues with songs of joy.
Then it was said among the nations,
"The Lord has done great things for them."
The Lord has done great things for us,
And we are filled with joy.
Those who sow with tears will reap with
   songs of joy.
Those who go out weeping, carrying seed to
   sow,
Will return with songs of joy, carrying
   sheaves with them.
   (Psalm 126:1–3 and 5–6, NIV)

However, it didn't take Pharaoh long to return to his wicked ways. The Egyptian peoples' sufferings had subsided, so their leader decided that he had made a huge mistake. Pharaoh promptly called for his entire army to pursue the Israelites, intending to re-capture them.

When the king of Egypt was told that the people had fled, Pharaoh and his officials changed their minds about them and said, "What have we done? We have let the Israelites go and have lost their services!"

So he had his chariot made ready and took his army with him. He took six hundred of the best chariots, along with all the other chariots of Egypt, with officers over all of them. The Lord hardened the heart of Pharaoh King of Egypt, so that he pursued the

Israelites, who were marching out boldly. The Egyptians—all Pharaoh's horses and chariots, horsemen and troops—pursued the Israelites and overtook them as they camped by the sea near Pi Hahiroth, opposite Baal Zephon.

As Pharaoh approached, the Israelites looked up, and there were the Egyptians, marching after them. They were terrified and cried out to the Lord. They said to Moses, "Was it because there were no graves in Egypt that you brought us to the desert to die? What have you done to us by bringing us out of Egypt? Didn't we say to you in Egypt, 'Leave us alone; let us serve the Egyptians'? It would have been better for us to serve the Egyptians than to die in the desert!"

Moses answered the people, "Do not be afraid. Stand firm and you will see the deliverance the Lord will bring you today. The Egyptians you see today you will never see again. The Lord will fight for you; you need only to be still" (Exodus 14:5–14, NIV).

In this lies an important truth:

*On our journey of faith, the most dangerous times
may not be during the heat of the battle, but
immediately following our major victories.*

And, from God's word, "Stay alert! Watch out for
your great enemy, the devil. He prowls around like a
roaring lion looking for someone to devour. Stand firm
against him and be strong in your faith" (1 Peter 5:8–9,
NLT).

This is an invaluable reminder to maintain a strong
defense at all times, perhaps especially when enjoying the
first flush of victory. We need to protect ourselves from
being blindsided by an adversary hoping to take advantage of our jubilant state. Pharaoh's sneak attack took the
Israelites completely by surprise, striking terror into their
hearts. Shamefully, God's people panicked.

Similarly, we must remain prayerful at all times.
Although we can empathize with the Israelites' terror at
the sight of their former—and formidable—Egyptian
oppressors, it is still disheartening that God's people all
but abandoned faith in Him. They had already experienced so many miracles from God before leaving Egypt
that it's hard to believe that their faith would have melted,
like ice cream in the sun, when faced with trouble. The
Hebrew people seemed to have had more faith in their
enemy's ability to harm them than in God's ability to

protect them! This level of ingratitude and disbelief begs the question:

How much does God have to do before
we can believe in Him?

"Don't be afraid," the prophet answered. "Those who are with us are more than those who are with them" (2 Kings 6:16, NIV).

But you belong to God, my dear children. You have already won a victory over those people, because the Spirit who lives in you is greater than the spirit who lives in the world (1 John 4:4, NLT).

God had just succeeded in delivering them from four hundred years of slavery, yet they still regretted following Him. Not even personally witnessing some of God's most awesome acts was enough to convince His own people! To be honest, had I been God, at this point I'd have felt tempted to let Pharaoh have them back, especially after they complained, "What have you done to us by bringing us out of Egypt?" (Exodus 14:11, NIV).

Fear had completely mastered them, of course, reminding us that not even *firsthand* experience of God's miracles is enough to produce faith. Instead, the Hebrews, confronted with a fresh crisis, surrendered almost all of their faith in God. It would take another word from God, through His servant Moses, to restore their faith in Him.

> Then the Lord said to Moses, "Why are you crying out to me? Tell the Israelites to move on. Raise your staff and stretch out your hand over the sea to divide the water so that the Israelites can go through the sea on dry ground. I will harden the hearts of the Egyptians so that they will go in after them. And I will gain glory through Pharaoh and all his army, through his chariots and his horsemen. The Egyptians will know that I am the Lord when I gain glory through Pharaoh, his chariots and his horsemen."
>
> Then the angel of God, who had been traveling in front of Israel's army, withdrew and went behind them. The pillar of cloud also moved from in front and stood behind them, coming between the armies of Egypt and Israel. Throughout the night the cloud brought darkness to the one side and light to the other side; so neither went near the other all night long.
>
> Then Moses stretched out his hand over the sea, and all that night the Lord drove the sea back with a strong east wind and turned it into dry land. The waters were divided, and the

Israelites went through the sea on dry ground, with a wall of water on their right and on their left.

The Egyptians pursued them, and all Pharaoh's horses and chariots and horsemen followed them into the sea. During the last watch of the night the Lord looked down from the pillar of fire and cloud at the Egyptian army and threw it into confusion. He jammed the wheels of their chariots so that they had difficulty driving. And the Egyptians said, "Let's get away from the Israelites! The Lord is fighting for them against Egypt."

Then the Lord said to Moses, "Stretch out your hand over the sea so that the waters may flow back over the Egyptians and their chariots and horsemen."

Moses stretched out his hand over the sea, and at daybreak the sea went back to its place. The Egyptians were fleeing towards it, and the Lord swept them into the sea. The water flowed back and covered the chariots and horsemen— the entire army of Pharaoh that had followed the Israelites into the sea. Not one of them survived.

But the Israelites went through the sea on dry ground, with a wall of water on their right and on their left. That day the Lord saved Israel from the hands of the Egyptians, and Israel saw the Egyptians lying dead on the shore. And when the Israelites saw the mighty hand of the Lord displayed against the Egyptians, the people feared the Lord and put their trust in him and in Moses his servant (Exodus 14:15–31, NIV).

Human nature tends to lean more toward celebration than toward preparation. Similarly, it's when we are in most need of God that we tend to seek Him most fervently. This is not a wise way to live. It's far better to practice the ongoing protocols that keep faith strong by spending daily quality time with God throughout both good and bad times. And as a wise person once said, *"If you only pray when you're in trouble, you're in trouble."*

"Keep alert at all times" (Luke 21:36, NLT). In short, although you may be in the enviable position of having just won a major victory, as the Israelites had, you still need to prioritize spiritual vigilance as part of your journey of faith. We need to respond effectively to challenges and to make quicker comebacks if our faith is prepared to receive fresh guidance from God. Don't allow yourself to be robbed of all that you've fought for, as the Israelites almost did, by letting down your spiritual guard.

Worthy champions never allow themselves to become
casual or lazy, lest they lose their crowns.

Even when feeling most jubilant over your victories, be on the lookout for surprise attacks. Practice the discipline of abiding in God's word on a daily basis and be continually thankful for all that He has already done for us. Establishing and fostering a regular pattern of speaking with and listening to Him in prayer will strengthen us and make us ready for anything.

Hold tight to your trust in God. Remember, in the same way that we obtain our victories, we will maintain them. Former British Prime Minister Margaret Thatcher once said, "You may have to fight a battle more than once to win it!" And Irish orator John Philpot Curran famously remarked, "The price of freedom is eternal vigilance."

Of course, the Israelites went on to win their final battle with Pharaoh, but not before letting their fears almost rob them of their hard-won freedom. The takeaway? Leave no room for pride on your faith journey, for this may lead to defeat or destruction. "Pride goes before destruction, a haughty spirit before a fall (Proverbs 16:18, NIV).

We are God's creation and He is our source. Humbling ourselves and maintaining a strong and trusting daily connection with Him should prevent our responding to His immense kindness with unbelief, as the

Israelites did. "For in him we live and move and exist" (Acts 17:28, NLT).

> *It's also true that faith is a lifestyle, not an event. If uncertain about how to proceed in your own walk with God, always ask Him for wisdom.*

If you need wisdom, ask our generous God, and he will give it to you. He will not rebuke you for asking. But when you ask him, be sure that your faith is in God alone. Do not waver, for a person with divided loyalty is as unsettled as a wave of the sea that is blown and tossed by the wind. Such people should not expect to receive anything from the Lord (James 1:5–7, NLT).

"I am the vine; you are the branches. If you remain in me and I in you, you will bear much fruit; apart from me you can do nothing" (John 15:5, NIV).

God has promised to be with us throughout all the vicissitudes of life. Therefore, try not to waver or to possess divided loyalties. Be God-honoring at all times and in all things, no matter what life throws at you. The Scriptures also remind us to be strong in the Lord and in his mighty power. Put on all of God's armor so that you will be able to stand firm against all strategies of the devil. For we are not fighting against flesh-and-blood enemies, but against evil rulers and authorities of the unseen world, against mighty powers in this dark world, and against evil spirits in the heavenly places.

Therefore, put on every piece of God's armor so you will be able to resist the enemy in the time of evil. Then after the battle you will still be standing firm. Stand your ground, putting on the belt of truth and the body armor of God's righteousness. For shoes, put on the peace that comes from the Good News so that you will be fully prepared. In addition to all of these, hold up the shield of faith to stop the fiery arrows of the devil. Put on salvation as your helmet, and take the sword of the Spirit, which is the word of God.

Pray in the Spirit at all times and on every occasion. Stay alert and be persistent in your prayers for all believers everywhere (Ephesians 6:10–18, NLT).

Stay constantly vigilant and prayerful on the journey of faith. How vigilant and prayerful are you?

Chapter Seven

"WHERE'S THE BEEF?"

May I never forget the good

things he does for me.

—PSALM 103:2 (NLT)

After the fierce final battle with the Egyptians, the Israelites continued on their journey toward their promised real estate from God. It was guaranteed to be a land prosperous and full of blessings. All that would be required was to follow God's instructions through His servant Moses, although God had also placed Aaron and Miriam alongside Moses, as leaders over the people. (See Micah 6:4.)

> So I have come down to rescue them from the power of the Egyptians and lead them out of Egypt into their own fertile and spacious land. It is a land flowing with milk and honey—the land where the Canaanites, Hittites, Amorites,

Perizzites, Hivites, and Jebusites now live. (Exodus 3:8, NLT).

So obey the commands of the LORD your God by walking in his ways and fearing him. For the LORD your God is bringing you into a good land of flowing streams and pools of water, with fountains and springs that gush out in the valleys and hills. It is a land of wheat and barley; of grapevines, fig trees, and pomegranates; of olive oil and honey. It is a land where food is plentiful and nothing is lacking. It is a land where iron is as common as stone, and copper is abundant in the hills. When you have eaten your fill, be sure to praise the LORD your God for the good land he has given you.

"But that is the time to be careful! Beware that in your plenty you do not forget the LORD your God and disobey his commands, regulations, and decrees that I am giving you today. For when you have become full and prosperous and have built fine homes to live in, and when your flocks and herds have become very large and your silver and gold have multiplied along with everything else, be careful! Do not become proud at that time and forget the LORD your God, who rescued you from slavery in the land of Egypt (Deuteronomy 8:6–14, NLT).

However, things began to go horribly wrong when the people began to complain bitterly against God, and all because of the food!

Then the whole community of Israel set out from Elim and journeyed into the wilderness of Sin, between Elim and Mount Sinai. They arrived there on the fifteenth day of the second month, one month after leaving the land of Egypt. There, too, the whole community of Israel complained about Moses and Aaron. "If only the Lord had killed us back in Egypt," they moaned. "There we sat around pots filled with meat and ate all the bread we wanted. But now you have brought us into this wilderness to starve us all to death."

Then the Lord said to Moses, "Look, I'm going to rain down food from heaven for you. Each day the people can go out and pick up as much food as they need for that day. I will test them in this to see whether or not they will follow my instructions. On the sixth day they will gather food, and when they prepare it, there will be twice as much as usual."

So Moses and Aaron said to all the people of Israel, "By evening you will realize it was the Lord who brought you out of the land of Egypt. In the morning you will see the glory of the Lord, because he has heard your complaints, which are against him, not against us. What have we done that you should complain about us?"

Then Moses added, "The Lord will give you meat to eat in the evening and bread to satisfy you in the morning, for he has heard all your complaints against him. What have we done? Yes, your complaints are against the Lord, not against us."

Then Moses said to Aaron, "Announce this to the entire community of Israel: 'Present yourselves before the Lord, for he has heard your complaining.'" And as Aaron spoke to the whole community of Israel, they looked out toward the wilderness. There they could see the awesome glory of the Lord in the cloud. Then the Lord said to Moses, "I have heard the Israelites' complaints. Now tell them, 'In the evening you will have meat to eat, and in the morning you will have all the bread you want. Then you will know that I am the Lord your God.'" That evening vast numbers of quail flew in and covered the camp. And the next morning the area around the camp was wet with dew. When the dew evaporated, a flaky substance as fine as frost blanketed the ground. The Israelites were puzzled when they saw it. "What is it?" they asked each other. They had no idea what it was. And Moses told them, "It is the food the Lord has given you to eat" (Exodus 16:1–15, NLT).

Soon the people began to complain about their hardship, and the LORD heard everything they said. Then the LORD's anger blazed against them, and he sent a fire to rage among them, and he destroyed some of the people in the outskirts of the camp. Then the people screamed to Moses for help, and when he prayed to the LORD, the fire stopped. After that, the area was known as Taberah (which means "the place of burning"), because fire from the LORD had burned among them there.

The foreign rabble who were traveling with the Israelites began to crave the good things of Egypt. And the people of Israel also began to complain. "Oh, for some meat!" they exclaimed. "We remember the fish we used to eat for free in Egypt. And we had all the cucumbers, melons, leeks, onions, and garlic we wanted. But now our appetites are gone. All we ever see is this manna!"

The manna looked like small coriander seeds, and it was pale yellow like gum resin. The people would go out and gather it from the ground. They made flour by grinding it with hand mills or pounding it in mortars. Then they boiled it in a pot and made it into flat cakes. These cakes tasted like pastries baked with olive oil. The manna came down on the camp with the dew during the night.

Moses heard all the families standing in the doorways of their tents whining, and the Lord became extremely angry. Moses was also very aggravated. And Moses said to the Lord, "Why are you treating me, your servant, so harshly? Have mercy on me! What did I do to deserve the burden of all these people? Did I give birth to them? Did I bring them into the world? Why did you tell me to carry them in my arms like a mother carries a nursing baby? How can I carry them to the land you swore to give their ancestors? Where am I supposed to get meat for all these people? They keep whining to me, saying, 'Give us meat to eat!' I can't carry all these people by myself! The load is far too heavy! If this is how you intend to treat me, just go ahead and kill me. Do me a favor and spare me this misery!" (Numbers 11:1–15, NLT).

God had blessed the Israelites with a perfect and heavenly diet to keep them strong on their journey but, according to the people, it was less tasty than what they'd been used to eating in captivity. These ungrateful people even dared to complain that there wasn't enough beef or bread for their tastes. (Well, I never! Be honest, am I the only one resisting the urge to smack these people? God had singlehandedly delivered them from over four hundred years of slavery and supplied them with divine nutrition. In return for His generosity, the Israelites could only respond with grumbling. The old saying that we should count our blessings and not our problems was coined for this circumstance!)

However, *we can all fall into the trap of murmuring against God if we lose our sense of gratitude toward Him.*

After all that God had so generously done for them, the Israelites ought to have been amazingly thankful. Instead, they murmured against God for what they had *not yet* received. While it may be tempting to give in to the habit of complaint, the Hebrew people's behavior serves as an important reminder that *grumbling against God is a sin and dangerous to our faith.*

Nothing worth having ever comes easily, so we must be extremely careful not to fall into discontent or to begin to doubt our Creator's existence, abilities, and love. The Scriptures teach us that our needs are always on God's mind and that He is constantly thinking of new ways to bless us.

How precious are your thoughts about me, O God. They cannot be numbered! I can't even count them; they outnumber the grains of sand! And when I wake up, you are still with me! (Psalm 139:17–18, NLT).

Are not five sparrows sold for two pennies? Yet not one of them is forgotten by God. Indeed, the very hairs of your head are all numbered. Don't be afraid; you are worth more than many sparrows (Luke 12:6–7, NIV).

Exercising patience and gratitude while waiting for more of God's promises to manifest in our lives is an important key to living a life of faith. (See Hebrews 6:12.)

But despite their failings, God still treasured and loved the Hebrews and took full responsibility for their needs. A faithful and forgiving God, He continued to bless the Israelites even when they displeased Him. When you consider all that God did for them, you'd have imagined that they would have needed no additional incentive to praise and thank Him. Instead, they kept on complaining: "But the people were thirsty for water there, and they grumbled against Moses. They said, 'Why did you bring us up out of Egypt to make us and our children and livestock die of thirst?'" (Exodus 17:3, NIV).

Does this, possibly, ring any bells? Have you ever experienced people for whom you have done much, yet they still badmouth or even betray you? How would you have liked to be the leader of such an ungrateful bunch? Imagine how furious God must have been! The final straw finally came when the Israelites were about to possess their very own, God-given, Promised Land. They were about eleven days' journey away when their leaders asked them to prepare to enter into their inheritance. It was then, believe it or not, that the worst examples of their grumbling, complaining and faithlessness surfaced: "The Lord said to Moses, "Send some men to explore the land of Canaan, which I am giving to the Israelites" Numbers 13:1–2, NIV).

So they went up and explored the land from the Desert of Zin as far as Rehob, toward Lebo Hamath . . . . When they reached the Valley of Eshkol, they cut off a branch bearing a single cluster of grapes. Two of them carried it on a pole between them, along with some pomegranates and figs. That place was called the Valley of Eshkol because of the cluster of grapes the Israelites cut off there. At the end of forty days they returned from exploring the land.

They came back to Moses and Aaron and the whole Israelite community at Kadesh in the Desert of Paran. There they reported to them and to the whole assembly and showed them the fruit of the land. They gave Moses this account: "We went into the land to which you sent us, and it does flow with milk and honey! Here is its fruit. But the people who live there are powerful, and the cities are fortified and very large. We even saw descendants of Anak there. The Amalekites live in the Negev; the Hittites, Jebusites and Amorites live in the hill country; and the Canaanites live near the sea and along the Jordan."

Then Caleb silenced the people before Moses and said, "We should go up and take possession of the land, for we can certainly do it."

But the men who had gone up with him said, "We can't attack those people; they are stronger than we are." And they spread among the Israelites a bad report about the land they had explored. They said, "The land we explored devours those living in it. All the people we saw there are of great size. We saw the Nephilim there (the descendants of Anak come from the Nephilim). We seemed like grasshoppers in our own eyes, and we looked the same to them" (Numbers 13:21–33, NIV).

All the Israelites grumbled against Moses and Aaron, and the whole assembly said to them, "If only we had died in Egypt! Or in this wilderness!" . . . And they said to each other, "Let us appoint a leader and return to Egypt." . . . Joshua son of Nun and Caleb son of Jephunneh, who were among those who had spied out the land, tore their clothes and said to the whole congregation of Israel, "The land we passed through and explored is an exceedingly good land. If the LORD delights in us, He will bring us into this land, a land flowing with milk and honey, and He will give it to us. Only do not rebel against the LORD, and do not be afraid of the people of the land, for they will be like bread for us. Their protection has been removed, and the LORD is with us. Do not be afraid of them!" But the entire congregation threatened to stone Joshua and Caleb.

The Lord said to Moses, "How long will these people treat me with contempt? How long will they refuse to believe in me, in spite of all the signs I have performed among them" (Numbers 14:2, 4, 6–11, NIV).

The Lord replied, "I have forgiven them, as you asked. Nevertheless, as surely as I live and as surely as the glory of the Lord fills the whole earth, not one of those who saw my glory and the signs I performed in Egypt and in the wilderness but who disobeyed me and tested me ten times—not one of them will ever see the land I promised on oath to their ancestors. No one who has treated me with contempt will ever see it. But because my servant Caleb has a different spirit and follows me wholeheartedly, I will bring him into the land he went to, and his descendants will inherit it (Numbers 14:20–24, NIV).

The Lord said to Moses and Aaron: "How long will this wicked community grumble against me? I have heard the complaints of these grumbling Israelites. So tell them, 'As surely as I live, declares the Lord, I will do to you the very thing I heard you say: In this wilderness your bodies will fall—every one of you twenty years old or more who was counted in the census and who has grumbled against me.

Not one of you will enter the land I swore with uplifted hand to make your home, except Caleb son of Jephunneh and Joshua son of Nun. As for your children that you said would be taken as plunder, I will bring them in to enjoy the land you have rejected. But as for you, your bodies will fall in this wilderness. Your children will be shepherds here for forty years, suffering for your unfaithfulness, until the last of your bodies lies in the wilderness. For forty years— one year for each of the forty days you explored the land—you will suffer for your sins and know what it is like to have me against you.' I, the

Lord, have spoken, and I will surely do these things to this whole wicked community, which has banded together against me. They will meet their end in this wilderness; here they will die" (Numbers 14:26–35, NIV).

Now, moaning and grumbling against God counts as rebellion, which is a very serious charge. The Merriam-Webster dictionary describes "rebellion" as "an opposition, open resistance to or defiance to one in authority."

Grievances are generally the cause for a rebellion, but the Israelites had no just cause to rebel against God. Instead, they had so repeatedly disobeyed Him that God had even asked His people, "My people, what have I done to you? How have I been a burden to you? Answer me. I brought you out of Egypt; I rescued you from slavery" (Micah 6:3–4, GNT).

God loves human beings and has fully proven this by sending His son to suffer and die in our place, taking all the punishment for our sins. "God showed his great love for us by sending Christ to die for us while we were still sinners" (Romans 5:8, NLT).

He also promises us in His word that "Neither height nor depth, nor anything else in all creation, will be able to separate us from the love of God that is in Christ Jesus our Lord" (Romans 8:39, NIV).

There is never any justifiable reason to act defiantly or rebelliously toward God. He cannot work on our behalf when we respond with faithlessness and grumbling. As it was written, "Because of their unbelief, he couldn't do any miracles among them except to place his hands on a few sick people and heal them" (Mark 6:5, NLT).

We may think that doubting God or complaining against Him isn't all that serious. But these two dangerous habits still have the potential to rob us of many blessings stored up for us by God. Instead, we need to respond with love and unwavering faith toward Him and gratefully receive all that He has for us.

> The thief comes only to steal and kill and destroy; I have come that they may have life, and have it to the full. I am the good shepherd. The good shepherd lays down his life for the sheep (John 10:10–11, NIV).

Many families, relationships, businesses, and even nations have failed because people have indulged in these sinful habits. But we need to learn from the Israelites' folly and make a determined effort to resist every temptation to dishonor and disobey God. The Hebrews repeatedly revealed their lack of faith in God through their despicable behavior—and it almost cost them their "promised land."

> And who was it who rebelled against God, even though they heard his voice? Wasn't it the people Moses led out of Egypt? And who made God angry for forty years? Wasn't it the people who sinned, whose corpses lay in the wilderness? And to whom was God speaking when he took an oath that they would never enter his rest? Wasn't it the people who disobeyed him? So we see that because of their unbelief they were not able to enter his rest (Hebrews 3:16–19, NLT).

What negative behavior patterns do you indulge in?

Are you willing to repent and surrender these to receive God's promised blessings?

Chapter Eight

RISE ABOVE THE BEEF

*And if a household is divided against
itself, that household won't stand.*
—MARK 3:25 (ISV)

We're also warned in the Scriptures about another grave danger to our faith: strife. Quarreling, bickering, and wrangling amongst ourselves disrupts harmony and causes divisions, which can hinder the effective working of our faith. The fuel of faith is love and love needs a harmonious environment in order to thrive.

For in Christ Jesus neither circumcision nor uncircumcision counts for anything, but only faith working through love (Galatians 5:6, ESV).

Three things will last forever—faith, hope, and
love—and the greatest of these is love (1 Corinthians 13:13, NLT).

Genuine biblical faith is *always* expressed through
love. So we must prevent strife from taking hold as much
as humanly possible. By putting a swift end to strife
whenever it rears its ugly head, we can prevent our relationship with God and others from turning sour.

Starting a quarrel is like opening a floodgate,
so stop before a dispute breaks out (Proverbs
17:14, NLT).

It is to one's honor to avoid strife, but every fool
is quick to quarrel (Proverbs 20:3, NIV).

Whenever we choose to harbor hatred, envy, unfor-
giveness, etc., toward others, it obstructs the smooth
working of our faith. Thinking and acting in this way is
not love. However, forgiving those who have wronged us
is part of how we allow God's kind of love—agape—to
flow through us to others. Agape is the selfless, sacrificial,
unconditional love that pours from God, powers up our
faith, and preserves Christian unity. Agape brings God's
blessings into our lives.

"Have faith in God," Jesus answered. "Truly I tell you, if anyone says to this mountain, 'Go, throw yourself into the sea,' and does not doubt in their heart but believes that what they say will happen, it will be done for them. Therefore I tell you, whatever you ask for in prayer, believe that you have received it, and it will be yours. And when you stand praying, if you hold anything against anyone, forgive them, so that your Father in heaven may forgive you your sins" (Mark 11:22–25, NIV).

How good and pleasant it is when God's people live together in unity! It is like precious oil poured on the head, running down on the beard, running down on Aaron's beard, down on the collar of his robe. It is as if the dew of Hermon were falling on Mount Zion. For there the Lord bestows his blessing, even life forevermore (Psalm 133:1–3, NIV).

In a previous book, *Giving God Ultimate Love: Over-the-Top Mega Love,* I shared how loving God made Jesus and many other believers in God demonstrate unshakeable faith in Him, which resulted in their receiving God's highest blessings. A life of faith must be based on true love for God, as well as for those people whom He has placed in our lives. Faith will only work when we keep our eyes on our love gauge, ensuring that it never runs low, and remembering that our Creator is love.

> Dear friends, let us continue to love one another, for love comes from God. Anyone who loves is a child of God and knows God. But anyone who does not love does not know God, for God is love. God showed how much he loved us by sending his one and only Son into the world so that we might have eternal life through him. This is real love—not that we loved God, but that he loved us and sent his Son as a sacrifice to take away our sins. Dear friends, since God loved us that much, we surely ought to love each other. No one has ever seen God. But if we love each other, God lives in us, and his love is brought to full expression in us (1 John 4:7–12, NLT).

We also need to stay humble. No one is immune to the danger of pride, the prime cause of unhappiness and dissent throughout the world. Disagreements often spring from our egotistical sense of superiority. This is not the way that love works! Strongly endeavor to avoid strife in your personal life and within your community.

The Scriptures also remind us not to let our own personal faith become a stumbling block to others. An illustration of this can be found in the New Testament, where some church members beefed amongst themselves—about beef!

> Now regarding your question about food that has been offered to idols. Yes, we know that "we all have knowledge" about this issue. But while knowledge makes us feel important, it is love that strengthens the church. Anyone who claims to know all the answers doesn't really know very much.
>
> But the person who loves God is the one whom God recognizes. So, what about eating meat that has been offered to idols? Well, we all know that an idol is not really a god and that there is only one God. There may be so-called gods both in heaven and on earth, and some people actually worship many gods and many lords. But for us, there is one God, the Father, by whom all things were created, and for whom we live. And there is one Lord, Jesus Christ, through whom all things were created, and through whom we live. However, not all believers know this. Some are accustomed to thinking of idols as being real, so when they eat food that has been offered to idols, they think of it as the worship of real gods, and their weak consciences are violated. It's true that we can't

win God's approval by what we eat. We don't
lose anything if we don't eat it, and we don't
gain anything if we do.

But you must be careful so that your freedom
does not cause others with a weaker conscience
to stumble. For if others see you—with your
"superior knowledge"—eating in the temple of
an idol, won't they be encouraged to violate their
conscience by eating food that has been offered
to an idol? So because of your superior knowledge, a weak believer for whom Christ died will
be destroyed. And when you sin against other
believers by encouraging them to do something
they believe is wrong, you are sinning against
Christ. So if what I eat causes another believer
to sin, I will never eat meat again as long as I
live—for I don't want to cause another believer
to stumble (1 Corinthians 8:1–13, NLT).

The arguments that arose in this church impacted
their faith so badly that it required the Apostle Paul to
resolve them. He brought the dissenting parties back
together and restored harmony within their faith community. Yet not even Paul was immune to the dangers of
strife and disagreement: he himself sustained a serious
falling-out with a companion in ministry with whom he
had worked closely for years. This had a very negative
impact on both of these servants of God.

Then Barnabas went to Tarsus to look for Saul, and when he found him, he brought him to Antioch. So for a whole year Barnabas and Saul met with the church and taught great numbers of people. The disciples were called Christians first at Antioch (Acts 11:25–26, NIV).

Now in the church at Antioch there were prophets and teachers: Barnabas, Simeon called Niger, Lucius of Cyrene, Manaen (who had been brought up with Herod the tetrarch) and Saul. While they were worshiping the Lord and fasting, the Holy Spirit said, "Set apart for me Barnabas and Saul for the work to which I have called them." So after they had fasted and prayed, they placed their hands on them and sent them off. The two of them, sent on their way by the Holy Spirit, went down to Seleucia and sailed from there to Cyprus. (Acts 13:1–4, NIV).

Some time later Paul said to Barnabas, "Let us go back and visit the believers in all the towns where we preached the word of the Lord and see how they are doing." Barnabas wanted to take John, also called Mark, with them, but Paul did not think it wise to take him, because he had deserted them in Pamphylia and had not continued with them in the work. They had such a sharp disagreement that they parted company. Barnabas took Mark and sailed for Cyprus, but Paul chose Silas and left, commended by the believers to the grace of the Lord. He went through Syria and Cilicia, strengthening the churches (Acts 15:36–41, NIV; see also Acts 9:26–27).

Strife and dissent represent a satanic trap, which we must avoid at all costs, as it can impact our faith and our service toward God and toward others. These two men were apparently never reconciled and—as far as New Testament records show—their evangelistic partnership seemed to come abruptly to an end. Paul, however, did later invite John Mark, the cause of their dispute, to accompany him on one of his many missionary journeys. They had obviously forgiven one another, as evidenced by this excerpt: "Only Luke is with me. Get Mark and bring him with you, because he is helpful to me in my ministry" (2 Timothy 4:11, NIV).

We may not always be able to undo damage done to relationships because of negative behaviors, but we *can* still endeavor to create new beginnings with those we have offended. This behavior is likeliest to succeed if we take full responsibility for our part in the discord and make no excuses, and if we seek forgiveness ourselves while trying to exercise forgiveness toward those who have hurt us. Paul and John Mark rose above their disagreement and were reunited. Let this inspire us to do the same! "Let love be your highest goal!" (1 Corinthians 14:1, NLT).

It's also important to remember that although we enjoy many benefits from relationships with others, those benefits are not the reason that we have relationships with them. The primary reason for loving God and others is because of who they are (their identities) not because of what they do for us (their usefulness). Having a relationship with anyone for the sake of any benefit conferred is not love. No one enjoys being pursued for the sake of possible benefits!

Always operating through love helps us to experience God's blessings in our lives, because our faith is birthed out of God's love for us. We display the DNA of our loving, heavenly parent when we unconditionally love Him and all those whom He has placed in our lives. Continuously examine your own heart to make sure that your love for God and others isn't running low, in order to ensure the effective working of your faith. Allow yourself to release the past. So many of the negative issues in our lives are the result of bad experiences! Don't let these bad roots bear any more fruit in your life; instead, always attempt to operate from love. Our personal relationships, faith communities, and even nations all desperately need this to happen. The entire world would greatly benefit if it did!

*Operating in love towards God and others
makes our faith work effectively.*

Are you keeping your eye on your love gauge?

Chapter Nine

FACE-OFF BETWEEN LIONS

*Submit yourselves, then, to God. Resist
the devil, and he will flee from you.*

—JAMES 4:7 (NLT)

Alone in a dark pit—at dead of night, entirely sur-
rounded by hungry lions—it looked like the end
of the road for Daniel.

He was originally from the tribe of Judah, in Israel,
and was only seventeen when he first came to Babylon.
This happened around 605 BC, and Israel had just lost a
brutal war with the mighty Babylonians, leaving Daniel
and many others exiled in Babylon.

> In the third year of the reign of Jehoiakim king
> of Judah, Nebuchadnezzar king of Babylon
> came to Jerusalem and besieged it. And the
> Lord delivered Jehoiakim king of Judah into
> his hand, along with some of the articles from

the temple of God. These he carried off to the temple of his god in Babylonia and put in the treasure house of his god.

Then the king ordered Ashpenaz, chief of his court officials, to bring into the king's service some of the Israelites from the royal family and the nobility—young men without any physical defect, handsome, showing aptitude for every kind of learning, well informed, quick to understand, and qualified to serve in the king's palace. He was to teach them the language and literature of the Babylonians. The king assigned them a daily amount of food and wine from the king's table. They were to be trained for three years, and after that they were to enter the king's service. Among those who were chosen were some from Judah: Daniel, Hananiah, Mishael and Azariah. The chief official gave them new names: to Daniel, the name Belteshazzar; to Hananiah, Shadrach; to Mishael, Meshach; and to Azariah, Abednego (Daniel 1:1–7 NIV).

The book of Daniel itself implies that Daniel was its author. (See Daniel 9:2 and 10:2.) Although some people view his story as fictional, this notion is contradicted by the prophet Ezekiel and even by Jesus, who both referred to Daniel as a real, historical personage. "The day is coming when you will see what Daniel the prophet spoke about—the sacrilegious object that causes desecration standing in the Holy Place" (Matthew 24:15, NLT). Reader, pay attention! (Jesus was quoting from Daniel 9:27, 11:31, and 12:11. See also Ezekiel 14:13–14 and 19–20.)

Daniel worked very hard to prove himself and soon became one of Babylon's highest-ranking officials. But his outstanding work ethic made him the target of envy. Some Babylonians saw him as a threat and launched a major attack against him.

Darius the Mede decided to divide the kingdom into 120 provinces, and he appointed a high officer to rule over each province. The king also chose Daniel and two others as administrators to supervise the high officers and protect the king's interests. Daniel soon proved himself more capable than all the other administrators and high officers. Because of Daniel's great ability, the king made plans to place him over the entire empire.

Then the other administrators and high officers began searching for some fault in the way Daniel was handling government affairs, but they couldn't find anything to criticize or condemn. He was faithful, always responsible, and completely trustworthy. So they concluded, "Our only chance of finding grounds for accusing Daniel will be in connection with the rules of his religion."

So the administrators and high officers went to the king and said, "Long live King Darius! We are all in agreement—we administrators, officials, high officers, advisers, and governors— that the king should make a law that will be strictly enforced. Give orders that for the next thirty days any person who prays to anyone, divine or human—except to you, Your Majesty—will be thrown into the den of lions. And now, Your Majesty, issue and sign this law so it cannot be changed, an official law of the Medes and Persians that cannot be revoked." So King Darius signed the law.

But when Daniel learned that the law had been signed, he went home and knelt down as usual in his upstairs room, with its windows open toward Jerusalem. He prayed three times a day, just as he had always done, giving thanks to his God. Then the officials went together to Daniel's house and found him praying and asking for God's help. So they went straight to the king and reminded him about his law. "Did you not sign a law that for the next thirty days any person who prays to anyone, divine or human—except to you, Your Majesty—will be thrown into the den of lions?"

"Yes," the king replied, "that decision stands; it is an official law of the Medes and Persians that cannot be revoked."

Then they told the king, "That man Daniel, one of the captives from Judah, is ignoring you and your law. He still prays to his God three times a day."

Hearing this, the king was deeply troubled, and he tried to think of a way to save Daniel. He spent the rest of the day looking for a way to get Daniel out of this predicament.

In the evening the men went together to the king and said, "Your Majesty, you know that according to the law of the Medes and the Persians, no law that the king signs can be changed."

So at last the king gave orders for Daniel to be arrested and thrown into the den of lions. The king said to him, "May your God, whom you serve so faithfully, rescue you."

A stone was brought and placed over the mouth of the den. The king sealed the stone with his own royal seal and the seals of his nobles, so that no one could rescue Daniel. Then the king returned to his palace and spent the night fasting. He refused his usual entertainment and couldn't sleep at all that night (Daniel 6:1–18, NLT).

When Daniel realized his danger, his first decision was to continue praying three times a day, as was his established pattern. Of course, many of us would pray fervently if suddenly confronted with danger—probably *all* of us! But who on earth gives glory and thanks to God when his life is about to be unjustly snuffed out? My own prayers would probably have been mostly cries for help! But Daniel had established a very strong bond with God before his crisis hit; he was still able to give thanks to God and glorify Him. We can all learn a great deal from his example.

Develop a daily habit of spending time in
God's presence before any crisis hits.

Remember, God has already won
victory over all our foes.

Our job is to simply trust in God and to resist every form of evil. The pattern of regular prayer set by Daniel reminds us to be fervent, grateful, and faithful, even in the midst of terrible adversity. Daniel's end appeared to be near, but Daniel continued to worship God, exactly as he always had.

The people who know their God shall stand firm
and take action (Daniel 11:32, ESV).

> Rejoice in the Lord always. I will say it again: Rejoice! (Philippians 4:4, NIV).

It's also noteworthy that, even though Daniel is often depicted as a young man in illustrations of this lion-den event in his life, he probably was over eighty at the time. His humility and courage seem even more valuable and admirable when you consider his age. Of course, as elders in the faith, our humility and heartfelt worship ought to deepen with age, and not diminish. In the book of Revelation, it was the elders who fell down prostrate to initiate worship to God, not the young. It's also wrong to believe that seniors have nothing significant to contribute in maturity. Leaving the most important aspects of our relationship with God to the leadership of the young, without full participation and guidance from seniors, is always an error.

> Surrounding the throne were twenty-four other thrones, and seated on them were twenty-four elders. They were dressed in white and had crowns of gold on their heads . . . . Whenever the living creatures give glory, honor and thanks to him who sits on the throne and who lives for ever and ever, the twenty-four elders fall down before him who sits on the throne and worship him who lives for ever and ever. They lay their crowns before the throne and say:

"You are worthy, our Lord and God, to receive glory and honor and power, for you created all things, and by your will they were created and have their being" (Revelation 4:4, 9–11, NLT).

And when he had taken it, the four living creatures and the twenty-four elders fell down before the Lamb. Each one had a harp and they were holding golden bowls full of incense, which are the prayers of God's people. And they sang a new song, saying: "You are worthy to take the scroll and to open its seals, because you were slain, and with your blood you purchased for God persons from every tribe and language and people and nation" (Revelation 5:8–9, NIV).

By His Holy Spirit, God lives *within* His redeemed children, and we can receive the grace to overcome at any age and at any stage of life. Daniel's example reminds us that being blessed to reach maturity is one of the highest blessings we can receive from God, and we should use it to share the message of His salvation with as many people as possible.

They will still bear fruit in old age, they will stay fresh and green, proclaiming, "The LORD is upright; he is my Rock, and there is no wickedness in him" (Psalm 92:14–15, NIV).

With long life I will satisfy him and show him
my salvation (Psalm 91:16, NIV).

One of Jesus' many titles is Lion of Judah, which
refers to His strength and majesty, as well as His being
an actual descendant of Judah. He is the one and only
true eternal king. (See Genesis 49:8–10 and Luke 1:33).
Lions are the kings of beasts and traditionally regarded
as symbols of power. They stand courageous and confi-
dent, always ready to attack or to defend, majestic and
awe-inspiring creatures. "The wicked run away when no
one is chasing them, but the godly are as bold as lions"
(Proverbs 28:1, NLT).

Another lion from the tribe of Judah, Daniel, is
about to teach us how to win against all odds, by plug-
ging into God's power.

Daniel refused to cave in to his fears, or to "sell out"
in order to save his own neck. Instead, Daniel prayed.
And Daniel's prayers were no knee-jerk reaction to
the massive trouble he was in; instead, they were part
of a long-established pattern. For many years prior to
the crisis of his life, Daniel's relationship with God had
always been his top priority.

This man of God fully demonstrated what it means
to *trust God at all times*. Although the wisdom and
strength of character emerging from age and experience is no longer as highly valued as in the past, Daniel
would leave his greatest legacy of faith as an elder, not

as a youth. His example also reminds us to strengthen our faith and connection with God *before* our hours of trial: this will give us the courage we need if suddenly confronted with danger. So how did God reward Daniel for his unshakeable faith?

Very early the next morning, the king got up and hurried out to the lions' den. When he got there, he called out in anguish, "Daniel, servant of the living God! Was your God, whom you serve so faithfully, able to rescue you from the lions?"

Daniel answered, "Long live the king! My God sent his angel to shut the lions' mouths so that they would not hurt me, for I have been found innocent in his sight. And I have not wronged you, Your Majesty."

The king was overjoyed and ordered that Daniel be lifted from the den. Not a scratch was found on him, for he had trusted in his God.

Then the king gave orders to arrest the men who had maliciously accused Daniel. He had them thrown into the lions' den, along with their wives and children. The lions leaped on them and tore them apart before they even hit the floor of the den.

Then King Darius sent this message to the people of every race and nation and language throughout the world: "Peace and prosperity to you! I decree that everyone throughout my kingdom should tremble with fear before the God of Daniel. For he is the living God, and he will endure forever. His kingdom will never be destroyed, and his rule will never end. He rescues and saves his people; he performs miraculous signs and wonders in the heavens and on earth. He has rescued Daniel from the power of the lions."

So Daniel prospered during the reign of Darius and the reign of Cyrus the Persian (Daniel 6:19–28, NLT).

It is easy to give thanks to God when things are going well. How many of us still do give thanks when the opposite is true?

There are all too many ways in which negative circumstances can arise in human lives but, on the other hand, if our faith is never challenged, we may never discover what we're really made of. Remember to hold tightly to your own faith as Daniel did, even in the midst of adversity. Fight the good fight and remember that you may be being recruited to receive a far greater blessing from God than you asked him for.

Apart from his usual prayers, Daniel fasted and also set aside additional times for special prayers when in need of guidance. His nation, Israel, often demonstrated ingratitude and rebelliousness toward God. So Daniel decided to seek God not just for his personal needs, but also for the deliverance of his nation.

Are we willing to do this for nations today
that have fallen far away from God?

Daniel's refusal to give up seeking God's help for his nation also reveals that if we're willing to press God for answers, He's more than willing to respond.

In the third year of the reign of King Cyrus of Persia, Daniel (also known as Belteshazzar) had another vision. He understood that the vision concerned events certain to happen in the future—times of war and great hardship.

When this vision came to me, I, Daniel, had been in mourning for three whole weeks. All that time I had eaten no rich food. No meat or wine crossed my lips, and I used no fragrant lotions until those three weeks had passed. On April 23, as I was standing on the bank of the great Tigris River, I looked up and saw a man dressed in linen clothing, with a belt of pure gold around his waist. His body looked like a precious gem. His face flashed like lightning, and his eyes flamed like torches. His arms and feet shone like polished bronze, and his voice roared like a vast multitude of people.

Only I, Daniel, saw this vision. The men with me saw nothing, but they were suddenly terrified and ran away to hide. So I was left there all alone to see this amazing vision. My strength left me, my face grew deathly pale, and I felt very weak. Then I heard the man speak, and when I heard the sound of his voice, I fainted and lay there with my face to the ground.

Just then a hand touched me and lifted me, still trembling, to my hands and knees. And the man said to me, "Daniel, you are very precious to God, so listen carefully to what I have to say to you. Stand up, for I have been sent to you." When he said this to me, I stood up, still trembling.

Then he said, "Don't be afraid, Daniel. Since the first day you began to pray for understanding and to humble yourself before your God, your request has been heard in heaven. I have come in answer to your prayer. But for twenty-one days the spirit prince of the kingdom of Persia blocked my way. Then Michael, one of the archangels, came to help me, and I left him there with the spirit prince of the kingdom of Persia. Now I am here to explain what will happen to your people in the future, for this vision concerns a time yet to come."

While he was speaking to me, I looked down at the ground, unable to say a word. Then the one who looked like a man touched my lips, and I opened my mouth and began to speak. I said to the one standing in front of me, "I am filled with anguish because of the vision I have seen, my lord, and I am very weak. How can someone like me, your servant, talk to you, my lord? My strength is gone, and I can hardly breathe."

Then the one who looked like a man touched me again, and I felt my strength returning. "Don't be afraid," he said, "For you are very precious to God. Peace! Be encouraged! Be strong!"

As he spoke these words to me, I suddenly felt stronger and said to him, "Please speak to me, my lord, for you have strengthened me." He replied, "Do you know why I have come? Soon I must return to fight against the spirit prince of the kingdom of Persia, and after that the spirit prince of the kingdom of Greece will come. Meanwhile, I will tell you what is written in the Book of Truth. (No one helps me against these spirit princes except Michael, your spirit prince) (Daniel 10:1–21, NLT).

Even after three weeks of fasting and daily seeking God, Daniel saw no visible results. But this man of faith persisted in prayer until he received God's answer. This pattern gives us another glimpse into the inner workings of true biblical faith.

Never give up on prayer, because a fierce spiritual battle may be taking place behind the scenes. God will always come through when we demonstrate unshakeable faith in Him.

God is rich in mercy. When He appears to be slow to hear, hold on even more tightly to your faith. We'll probably never know all that God is doing for us, but we need to continue to seek Him with all of our hearts, as Daniel did. Some of us might be facing terrible medical diagnoses or some other dire circumstances that make us feel almost as if we're caged in a lion's den. Others, all over the world, may be faced with plagues, wars, or some other serious threats to their nations. Remember that you can always count on God to come through, just as He did for Jochebed and Daniel. Remember the following verses from the Scriptures:

The light shines in the darkness, and the darkness can never extinguish it (John 1:5, NLT).

Yet I will rejoice in the LORD! I will be joyful in the God of my salvation! The Sovereign LORD is my strength! He makes me as sure-footed as a deer, able to tread upon the heights (Habakkuk 3:18–19, NLT).

Keep on asking, and you will receive what you ask for. Keep on seeking, and you will find. Keep on knocking, and the door will be opened to you (Matthew 7:7, NLT).

Daniel, Jochebed, and many others in the Bible knew and trusted God. They made up their minds not to be afraid but instead to resist evil with all their might. Begin your own walk with God—today! Grow to know and trust Him, as Jochebed did. Release all the pain of your past negative experiences to Him, as Daniel did when he was captured by the Babylonians and separated from his family, his people, and his nation. Human beings and human systems may fail us, but God will never fail us, and will ultimately cause all things to work together for our good.

Hold on to these truths, and on the other side of our struggles we'll have a far better understanding of why God led us in the ways that He did. His mercy and forgiveness are available to everyone willing to genuinely repent from their sins and to place their faith in Him.

It is also never too late to reach out to God or to get to know Him.

However, trusting in the sacrifice made by God's only begotten son, Jesus Christ, on the cross for all humankind's sins is the *only* way to receive the free and complete forgiveness that God offers.

God's ability to instantly, perfectly, and completely forgive was powerfully illustrated in the life of one of the two thieves who were crucified alongside Jesus. (See Luke 23:39–43.) If you restore your broken connection with God, you will find the path to victory. Daniel remained steadfast to the Lord to the end and served at least four kings in Babylon. Therefore, "Be strong, and let us fight bravely for our people and the cities of our God. The LORD will do what is good in his sight" (2 Samuel 10:12, NIV).

> *Daniel valued a close connection with*
> *God, which he nurtured daily.*

> *Do you seek God daily—or only when*
> *you desperately need Him?*

Chapter Ten

FAITH IN THE FACE
OF PERSECUTION

He told them: "Faithfully serve the LORD!"

—2 CHRONICLES 19:9

(*CONTEMPORARY ENGLISH VERSION*)

There were three other young men taken to Babylon from Judah at the same time as Daniel, Hananiah, Mishael, and Azariah. But once in Babylon, these were changed into the Babylonian names Shadrach, Meshach, and Abednego. (See Daniel 1:6–7). These men also shared Daniel's outstanding work ethic, so they were also favored by the king. All three were given official positions where they excelled, taking care of the provinces that they were assigned. But Shadrach, Meshach, and Abednego's faith was also to be severely tested. And the message to be drawn from their lives seems particularly poignant these days because of the increase in the persecution of Christians and acts of terrorism worldwide.

King Nebuchadnezzar made a gold statue ninety feet tall and nine feet wide and set it up on the plain of Dura in the province of Babylon. Then he sent messages to the high officers, officials, governors, advisers, treasurers, judges, magistrates, and all the provincial officials to come to the dedication of the statue he had set up. So all these officials came and stood before the statue King Nebuchadnezzar had set up.

Then a herald shouted out, "People of all races and nations and languages, listen to the king's command! When you hear the sound of the horn, flute, zither, lyre, harp, pipes, and other musical instruments bow to the ground to worship King Nebuchadnezzar's gold statue. Anyone who refuses to obey will immediately be thrown into a blazing furnace."

So at the sound of the musical instruments, all the people, whatever their race or nation or language, bowed to the ground and worshiped the gold statue that King Nebuchadnezzar had set up.

But some of the astrologers went to the king and informed on the Jews. They said to King Nebuchadnezzar, "Long live the king! You issued a decree requiring all the people to bow down and worship the gold statue when they hear the sound of the horn, flute, zither, lyre, harp, pipes, and other musical instruments. That decree also states that those who refuse to obey must be thrown into a blazing furnace. But there are some Jews—Shadrach, Meshach, and Abednego—whom you have put in charge of the province of Babylon. They pay no attention to you, Your Majesty. They refuse to serve your gods and do not worship the gold statue you have set up."

Then Nebuchadnezzar flew into a rage and ordered that Shadrach, Meshach, and Abednego be brought before him. When they were brought in, Nebuchadnezzar said to them, "Is it true, Shadrach, Meshach, and Abednego, that you refuse to serve my gods or to worship the gold statue I have set up? I will give you one more chance to bow down and worship the statue I have made when you hear the sound of the musical instruments. But if you refuse, you will be thrown immediately into the blazing furnace. And then what god will be able to rescue you from my power?"

Shadrach, Meshach, and Abednego replied, "O Nebuchadnezzar, we do not need to defend ourselves before you. If we are thrown into the blazing furnace, the God whom we serve is able to save us. He will rescue us from your power, Your Majesty. But even if he doesn't, we want to make it clear to you, Your Majesty, that we will never serve your gods or worship the gold statue you have set up.

Nebuchadnezzar was so furious with Shadrach, Meshach, and Abednego that his face became distorted with rage. He commanded that the furnace be heated seven times hotter than usual. Then he ordered some of the strongest men of his army to bind Shadrach, Meshach, and Abednego and throw them into the blazing furnace. So they tied them up and threw them into the furnace, fully dressed in their pants, turbans, robes, and other garments. And because the king, in his anger, had demanded such a hot fire in the furnace, the flames killed the soldiers as they threw the three men in. So Shadrach, Meshach, and Abednego, securely tied, fell into the roaring flames (Daniel 3:1–23, NLT).

As fear of terrorism and other acts of violence continue to mar life on earth, we need God's grace as much as ever. The courage to overcome adverse circumstances can only be obtained from God. If we were suddenly faced with the threat of violence, even death, for our faith—as Shadrach, Meshach, and Abednego were—God promises to give us the grace to triumph over evil.

When you are arrested and stand trial, don't worry in advance about what to say. Just say what God tells you at that time, for it is not you who will be speaking, but the Holy Spirit. "A brother will betray his brother to death, a father will betray his own child, and children will rebel against their parents and cause them to be killed. And everyone will hate you because you are my followers. But the one who endures to the end will be saved" (Mark 13:11–13, NLT).

Although these three young men faced death, they displayed exactly the same sort of backbone that Daniel and Jochebed did when confronted with great evil or grave danger. Shadrach, Meshach, and Abednego refused to deny their faith, thereby demonstrating not only their courage but also their great love for God. They clearly knew that earthly powers and governments will pass away and that only God's dominion will endure forever. These brave young men submitted to changes in their location, names, and diets, but flat out refused to have the God that they believed in and worshipped changed by the Babylonians.

So, stand firm in your own faith and be a light in your own sphere of influence.

Our Creator is the only one deserving worship and devotion, because our lives, all creation, and the many blessings that we enjoy are gifts to us from Him. Worshipping and serving God is an awesome privilege for human beings to have. Because: "The earth is the LORD's, and everything in it. The world and all its people belong to him" (Psalm 24:1, NLT).

So stay devoted to God. Great determination and courage may be needed in order to stay on the course of faith. These three displayed unshakeable faith in God under circumstances that, I trust, none of us will ever have to. And, as we learned from Daniel's own life story, staying connected with God as they did (through His word, worship, and daily prayer) will prepare us for any eventualities.

> *It's what we do on a regular basis that prepares us for life's most important moments.*

Shadrach, Meshach, and Abednego also ended up receiving a spectacular miracle from God.

Suddenly, Nebuchadnezzar jumped up in amazement and exclaimed to his advisers, "Didn't we tie up three men and throw them into the furnace?"

"Yes, Your Majesty, we certainly did," they replied.

"Look!" Nebuchadnezzar shouted. "I see four men, unbound, walking around in the fire unharmed! And the fourth looks like a god."

Then Nebuchadnezzar came as close as he could to the door of the flaming furnace and shouted: "Shadrach, Meshach, and Abednego, servants of the Most High God, come out! Come here!"

So Shadrach, Meshach, and Abednego stepped out of the fire. Then the high officers, officials, governors, and advisers crowded around them and saw that the fire had not touched them. Not a hair on their heads was singed, and their clothing was not scorched. They didn't even smell of smoke!

Then Nebuchadnezzar said, "Praise to the God of Shadrach, Meshach, and Abednego! He sent his angel to rescue his servants who trusted in him. They defied the king's command and were willing to die rather than serve or worship any god except their own God" (Daniel 3:24–28, NLT).

The three had possessed no foreknowledge that God would rescue them. Instead, they had simply resolved to live according to their convictions and felt at peace with whatever befell them. As politics heat up here on earth, I encourage all of us to be at peace similarly. We can trust in the all-sufficient grace of God, for His protection over us is assured.

> Those who live in the shelter of the Most
>   High will find rest in the shadow of the
>   Almighty.
> This I declare about the LORD:
> He alone is my refuge, my place of safety;
>   he is my God, and I trust him.
> For he will rescue you from every trap
>   and protect you from deadly disease.
> He will cover you with his feathers.
> He will shelter you with his wings.
> His faithful promises are your armor and
>   protection.
> Do not be afraid of the terrors of the night,
>   nor the arrow that flies in the day.
> Do not dread the disease that stalks in dark-
>   ness, nor the disaster that strikes at midday.
> Though a thousand fall at your side,
>   though ten thousand are dying around you,
>   these evils will not touch you.
> Just open your eyes,
>   and see how the wicked are punished.
> If you make the LORD your refuge,
>   if you make the Most High your shelter,
> no evil will conquer you;
>   no plague will come near your home.

For he will order his angels
    to protect you wherever you go.
They will hold you up with their hands
    so you won't even hurt your foot on a
    stone.
You will trample upon lions and cobras;
    you will crush fierce lions and serpents
    under your feet!
The LORD says, "I will rescue those who love
    me.
    I will protect those who trust in my name.
When they call on me, I will answer;
    I will be with them in trouble.
    I will rescue and honor them.
I will reward them with a long life
    and give them my salvation"
(Psalm 91:1–16, NLT).

My prayer for us all is that we shall be found faithful until the end.

If your faith is severely tested or even threatened, will you bow to the "god du jour" or will you honor the eternal and everlasting God with all that you have?

Chapter Eleven

THE CALM OF FAITH

By faith . . . women received back
their dead, raised to life again.
—HEBREWS 11:32, 35 (NIV)

"Get it together, Gina! Wake yourself up! Wake up! It's going to happen—it is, it's going to . . . Oh, someone, help me!

"This can't be real! Wake up, girl, wake up, wake up, wake up!"

These words were being hysterically repeated, over and over, by a young woman. She kept slapping herself as if trying to awaken from a nightmare.

Her young son lay on the hospital bed in front of her, a white bedsheet covering his face. The boy's grieving grandma, two silent medical staff, and several other weeping family members were in the room—but none of them could meet the mother's wild gaze.

A moment before, she had been so ecstatic. Still clutching her phone, wild hope surging in her soul, she had rushed into the room to tell her son that a matching bone marrow donor had been found—only to discover him dead.

People tried to comfort her, of course. The grandma tried to hug her, while the aunt rocked in her cousin's arms by the bed.

The senior nurse was herself deeply affected. She knew that poor Tim had been on the bone marrow transplant list for a long time. Cancer had weakened his young body, but with a transplant there had been hope. And now this! Even for the nurse it was heartbreaking. For his mother . . .

The senior nurse, tears running down her face, moved to close the door, knowing that every other patient—themselves living in dread—would be hearing the mother's anguish. Yet who could remain stoic in the face of such pain?

She thought: *Losing a child is the hardest—all those hopes and dreams snatched away. Of course she's inconsolable. All that anyone can do is to offer quiet support, and it doesn't feel like enough.* "Weep with those who weep" (Romans 12:15, NLT).

When three of Job's friends heard of the tragedy he had suffered, they got together and traveled from their homes to comfort and console him. Their names were

Eliphaz the Temanite, Bildad the Shuhite, and Zophar the Naamathite (Job 2:11, NLT).

I shared the previous scene—which I witnessed personally—to emphasize that the trauma of losing a child can never be overstated. It is unimaginably, almost unendurably, painful. The woman in our next lesson found herself in a somewhat similar situation. I want us to be able to connect with her, while drawing strength from her unshakeable faith.

> One day Elisha went on to Shunem, where a wealthy woman lived, who urged him to eat some food. So whenever he passed that way, he would turn in there to eat food. And she said to her husband, "Behold now, I know that this is a holy man of God who is continually passing our way. Let us make a small room on the roof with walls and put there for him a bed, a table, a chair, and a lamp, so that whenever he comes to us, he can go in there."
>
> One day he came there, and he turned into the chamber and rested there. And he said to Gehazi his servant, "Call this Shunammite." When he had called her, she stood before him. And he said to him, "Say now to her, 'See, you have taken all this trouble for us; what is to be done for you? Would you have a word spoken on

your behalf to the king or to the commander of the army?'" She answered, "I dwell among my own people." And he said, "What then is to be done for her?" Gehazi answered, "Well, she has no son, and her husband is old." He said, "Call her." And when he had called her, she stood in the doorway. And he said, "At this season, about this time next year, you shall embrace a son." And she said, "No, my lord, O man of God; do not lie to your servant." But the woman conceived, and she bore a son about that time the following spring, as Elisha had said to her.

When the child had grown, he went out one day to his father among the reapers. And he said to his father, "Oh, my head, my head!" The father said to his servant, "Carry him to his mother." And when he had lifted him and brought him to his mother, the child sat on her lap till noon, and then he died. And she went up and laid him on the bed of the man of God and shut the door behind him and went out. Then she called to her husband and said, "Send me one of the servants and one of the donkeys that I may quickly go to the man of God and come back again." And he said, "Why will you go to him today? It is neither new moon nor Sabbath." She said, "All is well." Then she saddled the donkey, and she said to her servant, "Urge the animal on; do not slacken the pace for me unless I tell you." So she set out and came to the man of God at Mount Carmel.

When the man of God saw her coming, he said to Gehazi his servant, "Look, there is the Shunammite. Run at once to meet her and say to her, 'Is all well with you? Is all well with your husband? Is all well with the child?'" And she answered, "All is well."

And when she came to the mountain to the man of God, she caught hold of his feet. And Gehazi came to push her away. But the man of God said, "Leave her alone, for she is in bitter distress, and the Lord has hidden it from me and has not told me." Then she said, "Did I ask my lord for a son? Did I not say, 'Do not deceive me'?" He said to Gehazi, "Tie up your garment and take my staff in your hand and go. If you meet anyone, do not greet him, and if anyone greets you, do not reply. And lay my staff on the face of the child." Then the mother of the child said, "As the Lord lives and as you yourself live, I will not leave you." So he arose and followed her. Gehazi went on ahead and laid the staff on the face of the child, but there was no sound or sign of life. Therefore he returned to meet him and told him, "The child has not awakened."

When Elisha came into the house, he saw the child lying dead on his bed. So he went in and shut the door behind the two of them and prayed to the Lord. Then he went up and lay on the child, putting his mouth on his mouth, his eyes on his eyes, and his hands on his hands. And as he stretched himself upon him, the flesh of the child became warm. Then he got up again and walked once back and forth in the house, and went up and stretched himself upon him. The child sneezed seven times, and the child opened his eyes. Then he summoned Gehazi and said, "Call this Shunammite." So he called her. And when she came to him, he said, "Pick up your son." She came and fell at his feet, bowing to the ground. Then she picked up her son and went out (2 Kings 4:8–37, ESV).

Of course, things don't always work out as we hope—or as they did in this inspiring instance. But this excerpt raises an important question: Are we willing to embrace God's omnipotence and, no matter how bad things look, to hold tightly to the truth that our loving heavenly father will bring us out on the other side?

The circumstances under which we may be called to demonstrate our own unshakeable faith in God may be completely different from the Shunammite's. But—in every case—God promises to work all things *for our good.* (See Romans 8:28.)

Regardless of what your personal faith challenge may be,

> *Take wise and decisive actions based on your own level of faith. This could make you the recipient of miracles that you could never have dreamed of.*

This courageous Shunammite may not have been entirely sure how things would turn out, but she demonstrated unshakeable faith by refusing to give in to her fears. We don't have the final say on the final picture in our own situations—although God does—but He always has the eternal in mind when responding to our prayers. For this reason, it's wonderfully wise to feed ourselves the daily nourishment of God's word and to practice those spiritual habits that shore up and cement our faith *before* adversity strikes. The grace to live a victorious life *in any circumstances* comes directly from God, if we are willing to open ourselves to Him.

At the opening of our discussion, we encountered Jochebed, a desperate mother who also wanted to save her son from his imminent death. The Shunammite woman however had an even more difficult task: bringing her already dead son back to life. When confronted with what would normally be an irreversible situation, both Jochebed and the Shunammite chose faith over fear. They decided on their courses of action and were able to rescue their children.

"What do you mean, 'If I can'?" Jesus asked. "Anything is possible if a person believes" (Mark 9:23, NLT).

Choosing faith over fear brings answers from God that far exceed anything that our imagination could come up with. These remarkable women show each of us how to operate in *the calm of unshakeable faith*. And when faith-filled mommas go to bat for their children, the impossible becomes possible! Of course, we're not the ones with the final say on how our challenges will end: God makes that call. But His supernatural power can be brought to any situation if we place our unwavering trust in Him. No one wants to endure one of life's worst nightmares, but this chapter poses this question:

Are you willing to place your full trust in God? Because if you are, you will receive more than you could ever imagine!

Chapter Twelve

"No Limits" Faith

Now to him who is able to do immeasurably
more than all we ask or imagine, according
to his power that is at work within us.

—Ephesians 3:20 (NIV)

The many miracles performed by Jesus gloriously illustrate how much our heavenly father loves us and longs to bless us. The next account reminds us that we can experience the "immeasurably more" of God in the most spectacular way, if we commit to belief in Him. One day Jesus and His disciples were busily doing God's business. No one, other than Jesus, was prepared for what God chose to do next.

> Now a man named Lazarus was sick. He was from Bethany, the village of Mary and her sister Martha. (This Mary, whose brother Lazarus now lay sick, was the same one who poured perfume on the Lord and wiped his feet with

her hair.) So the sisters sent word to Jesus, "Lord, the one you love is sick."

When he heard this, Jesus said, "This sickness will not end in death. No, it is for God's glory so that God's Son may be glorified through it." Now Jesus loved Martha and her sister and Lazarus. So when he heard that Lazarus was sick, he stayed where he was two more days, and then he said to his disciples, "Let us go back to Judea."

"But Rabbi," they said, "a short while ago the Jews there tried to stone you, and yet you are going back?"

Jesus answered, "Are there not twelve hours of daylight? Anyone who walks in the daytime will not stumble, for they see by this world's light. It is when a person walks at night that they stumble, for they have no light. "After he had said this, he went on to tell them, "Our friend Lazarus has fallen asleep; but I am going there to wake him up."

His disciples replied, "Lord, if he sleeps, he will get better." Jesus had been speaking of his death, but his disciples thought he meant natural sleep. So then he told them plainly, "Lazarus is dead, and for your sake I am glad I was not there, so that you may believe. But let us go to him."

Then Thomas (also known as Didymus) said to the rest of the disciples, "Let us also go, that we may die with him."

On his arrival, Jesus found that Lazarus had already been in the tomb for four days. Now Bethany was less than two miles from Jerusalem, and many Jews had come to Martha and Mary to comfort them in the loss of their brother. When Martha heard that Jesus was coming, she went out to meet him, but Mary stayed at home.

"Lord," Martha said to Jesus, "if you had been here, my brother would not have died. But I know that even now God will give you whatever you ask."

Jesus said to her, "Your brother will rise again."

Martha answered, "I know he will rise again in the resurrection at the last day."

Jesus said to her, "I am the resurrection and the life. The one who believes in me will live, even though they die; and whoever lives by believing in me will never die. Do you believe this?" "Yes, Lord," she replied, "*I believe* that you are the Messiah, the Son of God, who is to come into the world."

After she had said this, she went back and called her sister Mary aside. "The Teacher is here," she said, "and is asking for you." When

Mary heard this, she got up quickly and went
to him. Now Jesus had not yet entered the village, but was still at the place where Martha
had met him.

When the Jews who had been with Mary in
the house, comforting her, noticed how quickly
she got up and went out, they followed her,
supposing she was going to the tomb to mourn
there. When Mary reached the place where
Jesus was and saw him, she fell at his feet and
said, "Lord, if you had been here, my brother
would not have died."

When Jesus saw her weeping, and the Jews
who had come along with her also weeping,
he was deeply moved in spirit and troubled.
"Where have you laid him?" he asked.

"Come and see, Lord," they replied. Jesus
wept. Then the Jews said, "See how he loved
him!"

But some of them said, "Could not he who
opened the eyes of the blind man have kept
this man from dying?" Jesus, once more deeply
moved, came to the tomb. It was a cave with a
stone laid across the entrance. "Take away the
stone," he said.

"But, Lord," said Martha, the sister of the
dead man, "by this time there is a bad odor, for
he has been there four days."

Then Jesus said, "Did I not tell you that if you believe, you will see the glory of God?" [Emphasis added.]

So they took away the stone. Then Jesus looked up and said, "Father, I thank you that you have heard me. I knew that you always hear me, but I said this for the benefit of the people standing here, that they may believe that you sent me."

When he had said this, Jesus called in a loud voice, "Lazarus, come out!" The dead man came out, his hands and feet wrapped with strips of linen, and a cloth around his face. Jesus said to them,

"Take off the grave clothes and let him go" (John 11:1–44, NIV).

While Mary and her sister Martha were—for days—longing for Jesus to arrive and to heal their ailing brother, God had something still more surprising in mind. This family were God's chosen vessels to reveal that Jesus truly was the "resurrection and the life."

This "irreversible" situation was reversed, demonstrating the limitless nature of God's power!

Jesus' disciples had experienced Him as a healer on many occasions, but here God gave them a direct hint of what was to come: the resurrection of Jesus Christ from the dead—and, beyond that, a hint of what will happen eventually, when Jesus returns, when all who believed will also be raised from the dead, to dwell in God's presence forever. "For nothing will be impossible with God (Luke 1:37, ESV).

> *Will you place your unshakeable faith in God*
> *and experience His immeasurably more than*
> *all that you can ask for or imagine?*

Jairus' daughter

Another person of inspiring faith was a man called Jairus, whose simple but powerful belief produced the most spectacular result for his young daughter. This story proves that faith is really not complicated: it springs up naturally in hearts that believe in God's word.

> Jesus got into the boat again and went back to the other side of the lake, where a large crowd gathered around him on the shore. Then a leader of the local synagogue, whose name was Jairus, arrived. When he saw Jesus, he fell at his feet, pleading fervently with him. "My little daughter is dying," he said. "Please come and lay your hands on her; heal her so she can live." Jesus

went with him, and all the people followed, crowding around him (Mark 5:21–24, NLT).

While he was still speaking to her, messengers arrived from the home of Jairus, the leader of the synagogue. They told him, "Your daughter is dead. There's no use troubling the Teacher now."

But Jesus overheard them and said to Jairus, *"Don't be afraid. Just have faith"* [emphasis added].

Then Jesus stopped the crowd and wouldn't let anyone go with him except Peter, James, and John (the brother of James). When they came to the home of the synagogue leader, Jesus saw much commotion and weeping and wailing. He went inside and asked, "Why all this commotion and weeping? The child isn't dead; she's only asleep."

The crowd laughed at him. But he made them all leave, and he took the girl's father and mother and his three disciples into the room where the girl was lying. Holding her hand, he said to her, *"Talitha koum,"* which means "Little girl, get up!" And the girl, who was twelve years old, immediately stood up and walked around! They were overwhelmed and totally amazed. Jesus gave them strict orders not to tell anyone what had happened, and then he told them to give her something to eat (Mark 5:35–43, NLT).

When our faith is based on the truths that God shares in the Bible, His promises to us will surely come to pass, and having faith in God is the only way to bring His power to bear on a situation. The miraculous resurrection of Jairus' daughter reminds us that a key to receiving wonderful things from God, as taught by Jesus in this account, is, *"Don't be afraid. Just have faith."*

Hold tightly to your faith. Fiercely resist every temptation to cave in to fear and doubt. When it's required, wrestle with the enemy to prevent him from stealing killing or destroying what belongs to you.

"The thief comes only to steal and kill and destroy; I have come that they may have life, and have it to the full" (John 10:10, NIV). If you find yourself confronted with utter calamity or with any situation that seems likely to engulf you, hang on to your faith—even if it's the last thing left to you. This is the way to stay connected to the God who alone has the power to rescue us, restore us, and cause everything we endure to work together for our good.

When God's word inspires genuine faith in your heart, will you believe in Him and act upon it?

Chapter Thirteen

FAITH TO RELEASE

"I have told you these things, so that in me you may
have peace. In this world you will have trouble.
But take heart! I have overcome the world!"

—JOHN 16:33 (NIV)

There are times in our lives when we must stand our
ground and wrestle with the powers of darkness in
order to overcome the negative circumstances that we
face.

But there will also be times when things just don't
work out the way we hoped.

When the outcome of our struggles feels disappointing, this can place great strain on our faith. It requires
trust in God at the highest level to release our expectations. This aspect of faith is probably one of the hardest
for us to fully embrace. We need the discernment of the
Holy Spirit to recognize that

God's highest priority is to transform
us, not just our circumstances.

He may choose to grant us the grace to deal with circumstances as they are, rather than changing them for us. But, although we do not always understand God's ways, we need to remember that He will ultimately work everything out for our temporal *and our eternal* good. As we know, His ways are not our ways. To grow ever stronger in our faith, we will also need to recognize those times when the battle is not ours but the Lord's.

He said: "Listen, King Jehoshaphat and all who live in Judah and Jerusalem! This is what the LORD says to you: 'Do not be afraid or discouraged because of this vast army. For the battle is not yours, but God's'" (2 Chronicles 20:15, NIV). In other words, we need to learn when to wrestle with negative circumstances and when to yield them in complete trust in Him. Jesus knew when to release His own desires to God, even when He had to endure death on a cross.

> Jesus went out as usual to the Mount of Olives, and his disciples followed him. On reaching the place, he said to them, "Pray that you will not fall into temptation." He withdrew about a stone's throw beyond them, knelt down and prayed, "Father, if you are willing, take this cup from me; yet not my will, but yours be done."

An angel from heaven appeared to him and strengthened him. And being in anguish, he prayed more earnestly, and his sweat was like drops of blood falling to the ground (Luke 22:39–44, NIV).

Jesus surrendered all to God, by dying on a cross. This took the highest possible level of trust in God. Although things were not going the way in which Jesus wanted, although he prayed that "the cup might pass from me," He still released Himself completely to God, achieving the eternal salvation of us all. And all that we have to do is to place our trust in the sacrifice that He has already made for us. "He canceled the record of the charges against us and took it away by nailing it to the cross. In this way, he disarmed the spiritual rulers and authorities. He shamed them publicly by his victory over them on the cross" (Colossians 2:14–15, NLT). As with Moses, the fight over Jesus' life began just after His birth.

Jesus was born in Bethlehem, in Judea, during the reign of King Herod. About that time some wise men from eastern lands arrived in Jerusalem, asking, "Where is the newborn king of the Jews? We saw his star as it rose, and we have come to worship him."

King Herod was deeply disturbed when he heard this, as was everyone in Jerusalem. He called a meeting of the leading priests and teachers of religious law and asked, "Where is the Messiah supposed to be born?"

"In Bethlehem in Judea," they said, "for this is what the prophet wrote: 'And you, O Bethlehem in the land of Judah, are not least among the ruling cities of Judah, for a ruler will come from you who will be the shepherd for my people Israel'" (Matthew 2:1–6, NLT).

After the wise men were gone, an angel of the Lord appeared to Joseph in a dream. "Get up! Flee to Egypt with the child and his mother," the angel said. "Stay there until I tell you to return, because Herod is going to search for the child to kill him."

That night Joseph left for Egypt with the child and Mary, his mother, and they stayed there until Herod's death. This fulfilled what the Lord had spoken through the prophet: "I called my Son out of Egypt."

Herod was furious when he realized that the wise men had outwitted him. He sent soldiers to kill all the boys in and around Bethlehem who were two years old and under, based on the wise men's report of the star's first appearance (Matthew 2:13–16, NLT).

So King Herod, the ruler of Judea, heard about Jesus' birth and immediately wanted to kill him. One has to wonder why someone so powerful would consider a mere newborn such a threat. Perhaps the prophecies were the reason? At any rate, after successfully averting this danger, his parents returned to Israel, where Jesus began His earthly ministry. He walked perfectly before God, but was still subjected to severe persecution from men, as well as various tests and temptations from Satan. Each of these was an attempt to sabotage His mission. (See Matthew 4:1–11).

Through perfect obedience to God, Jesus ultimately won His every spiritual struggle and triumphantly completed His earthly purpose. Similarly, our greatest trials should produce blessings that will far surpass anything that we could have imagined. At least, they will if we trust in God and refuse to allow our faith to be shaken.

God's glory can be revealed, even through us, when we contend for our faith and refuse to surrender to the forces of darkness, but instead release our lives and circumstances to God, as Jesus did. We may not understand God's purposes, just as many heroes in the Bible may not have—yet they still demonstrated unshakeable faith in God.

How much more do I need to say? It would take too long to recount the stories of the faith of Gideon, Barak, Samson, Jephthah, David, Samuel, and all the prophets. By faith, these people overthrew kingdoms, ruled with justice, and received what God had promised them. They shut the mouths of lions, quenched the flames of fire, and escaped death by the edge of the sword. Their weaknesses were turned to strength. They became strong in battle and put whole armies to flight. Women received their loved ones back again from death.

But others were tortured, refusing to turn from God in order to be set free. They placed their hopes in better lives after the resurrection. Some were jeered at, and their backs were cut open with whips. Others were chained in prisons. Some died by stoning, some were sawed in half, and others were killed with the sword. Some went about wearing skins of sheep and goats, destitute and oppressed and mistreated. They were too good for this world, wandering over deserts and mountains, hiding in caves and holes in the ground. All these people earned good reputations because of their faith, yet none of them received all that God had promised.

> For God had something better in mind for us, so that they would not reach perfection without us (Hebrews 11:33–40, NLT).

> I consider that our present sufferings are not worth comparing with the glory that will be revealed in us (Romans 8:18, NIV).

Do you fully accept and believe this truth?

Paul

The Apostle Paul is credited with writing large portions of the New Testament, as well as with converting whole sections of the ancient world to Christianity. He also received wonderful revelations and supernatural visions from God, and was allowed to perform astonishing miracles: "God gave Paul the power to perform unusual miracles (Acts 19:11, NLT).

And yet, for reasons known only to God, Paul also suffered a long-standing ailment, from which he repeatedly begged God for relief. Instead, God told Paul that His grace must be sufficient.

> To keep me from being puffed up with pride because of the many wonderful things I saw, I was given a painful physical ailment, which acts as Satan's messenger to beat me and keep me from being proud. Three times I prayed to the Lord about this and asked him to take it away. But his answer was: "My grace is all you need, for my power is greatest when you are weak." I am most happy, then, to be proud of my weaknesses, in order to feel the protection of Christ's power over me. I am content with weaknesses,

insults, hardships, persecutions, and difficulties for Christ's sake. For when I am weak, then I am strong (2 Corinthians 12:7–10, GNT).

Paul had to exercise unwavering faith in God to deal with a situation that God would not change. Perhaps God in His loving wisdom knew that Paul had a vulnerability to pride which could have sabotaged all of his accomplishments? Or perhaps there was some other reason. However,

During times in our lives when we cannot understand God's actions, we must trust in His character: love.

Always remember that *everything* God does springs from His love. It would have been strange for Paul not to have sought God for healing, as he had seen God heal so many others. Paul knew exactly what God could do! But, although he could not understand the reason, Paul released himself, his pain, and his situation to God. He stopped wrestling with God's will for his life—exactly as Jesus had done—and received the grace from God to overcome through his own surrendering.

God's Holy Spirit, working within us, helps us to release our circumstances to God, even when we don't understand what He is doing.

Remember, God has promised to bring good out of *all* of our circumstances, the good and the bad, and to protect our hearts and minds with His peace. "Do not be anxious about anything, but in every situation, by prayer and petition, with thanksgiving, present your requests to God. And the peace of God, which transcends all understanding, will guard your hearts and your minds in Christ Jesus" (Philippians 4:6–7, NIV).

Remember, too, that when you place your trust in God, you are never on the losing side.

> We can rejoice, too, when we run into problems and trials, for we know that they help us develop endurance. And endurance develops strength of character, and character strengthens our confident hope of salvation. And this hope will not lead to disappointment. For we know how dearly God loves us, because he has given us the Holy Spirit to fill our hearts with his love (Romans 5:3–5, NLT).

> And through your faith, God is protecting you by his power until you receive this salvation, which is ready to be revealed on the last day for all to see.

> So be truly glad. There is wonderful joy ahead, even though you have to endure many trials for a little while. These trials will show

that your faith is genuine. It is being tested as fire tests and purifies gold—though your faith is far more precious than mere gold. So when your faith remains strong through many trials, it will bring you much praise and glory and honor on the day when Jesus Christ is revealed to the whole world (1 Peter 1:5–7, NLT).

Can anything ever separate us from Christ's love? Does it mean he no longer loves us if we have trouble or calamity, or are persecuted, or hungry, or destitute, or in danger, or threatened with death? (Romans 8:35, NLT).

No, in all these things we are more than conquerors through him who loved us. For I am convinced that neither death nor life, neither angels nor demons, neither the present nor the future, nor any powers, neither height nor depth, nor anything else in all creation, will be able to separate us from the love of God that is in Christ Jesus our Lord (Romans 8:37–40, NIV).

The presence of a debilitating ailment in Paul's body was no greater than God's grace in his life.

Will you still embrace God's grace if faced with some situation that you cannot understand?

Chapter Fourteen

FAITH TO WRESTLE

To this end I strenuously contend with all the
energy Christ so powerfully works in me.

—COLOSSIANS 1:29 (NIV)

During Jesus' earthly ministry, there was a woman who had suffered from constant hemorrhaging for many years. The woman had wrestled with her illness until her life savings were completely gone. The sickness had left her weak as well as bankrupt, but she refused to surrender hope, even though each day brought her new hardships. For example, there were the laws of uncleanness that she had to obey within her faith community.

If a woman has a flow of blood for many days that is unrelated to her menstrual period, or if the blood continues beyond the normal period, she is ceremonially unclean. As during her menstrual period, the woman will be unclean

as long as the discharge continues. Any bed she
lies on and any object she sits on during that
time will be unclean, just as during her normal
menstrual period. If any of you touch these
things, you will be ceremonially unclean. You
must wash your clothes and bathe yourself in
water, and you will remain unclean until evening
(Leviticus 15:25–27, NLT).

Her weakened state would also have deprived her
of most of the pleasures that we take for granted; even
cooking and dressing herself might have been impossible. At any rate, one day she decided to take the risk of
pressing through the massive crowds that followed Jesus,
in hopes of connecting her unshakeable faith with God's
healing power.

Jesus went with him, and all the people followed, crowding around him. A woman in the
crowd had suffered for twelve years with constant bleeding. She had suffered a great deal
from many doctors, and over the years she had
spent everything she had to pay them, but she
had gotten no better. In fact, she had gotten
worse. She had heard about Jesus, so she came
up behind him through the crowd and touched
his robe. For she thought to herself, "If I can just
touch his robe, I will be healed." Immediately

the bleeding stopped, and she could feel in her body that she had been healed of her terrible condition.

Jesus realized at once that healing power had gone out from him, so he turned around in the crowd and asked, "Who touched my robe?"

His disciples said to him, "Look at this crowd pressing around you. How can you ask, 'Who touched me?'" But he kept on looking around to see who had done it. Then the frightened woman, trembling at the realization of what had happened to her, came and fell to her knees in front of him and told him what she had done. And he said to her, "Daughter, your faith has made you well. Go in peace. Your suffering is over" (Mark 5:24–34, NLT).

Although this woman was in a severely weakened state, she refused to give up and continued to wrestle to find a solution to her desperate situation. From this we can learn that we must sometimes wrestle with our own fears and weaknesses to secure victories over the powers of darkness.

If it becomes necessary, will you wrestle with your circumstances until God's will—not Satan's—rules your life?

Chapter Fifteen

FAITH TO STAND

Be watchful, stand firm in the faith,
act like men, be strong.

—1 CORINTHIANS 16:13 (ESV)

In my previous two books (*I Made it Through and Giving God Ultimate Love: Over-the-Top Mega Love*), I made many references to Mary, the mother of Jesus. Her devotion to God motivated her to consent to whatever God called her to do. She went through many hardships so that the savior of the world could be born, and then she raised Him into adulthood.

Several additional lessons can be learned from Mary about having unshakeable faith in God. When Mary received the following— very troubling—prophecy from a respected man of God, there was no way that she could have understood what God had in mind. But she stood firmly on God's word and clung tightly to her faith. "Then Simeon blessed them and said to Mary, his mother: 'This child is destined to cause the falling and rising of many in Israel, and to be a sign that will be spoken against, so that the thoughts of many hearts will be revealed. And a sword will pierce your own soul too'" (Luke 2:34–35, NIV).

Mary's faith was severely tested early on during the escape to Egypt, undertaken in order to protect her baby son from Herod. Worst of all, she was forced to stand and watch as her miraculously conceived child was brutally put to death for crimes He had not committed. Mary accepted God's plan and purpose, even though she could not understand them. She could not have fully understood—at the time, at least—that her son was dying to save all humankind. But instead of insisting on a miraculous intervention from God, she trusted in Him and withstood Satan's onslaught against her family and her faith.

> Standing near the cross were Jesus' mother, and his mother's sister, Mary (the wife of Clopas), and Mary Magdalene. When Jesus saw his mother standing there beside the disciple he loved, he said to her, "Dear woman, here is your son." And he said to this disciple, "Here is your mother." And from then on this disciple took her into his home (John 19:25–27, NLT).

Surely *no one* could have fully understood, at the time, all that God was doing, despite the many prophecies beforehand. Mary's unique demonstration of faith really makes her humankind's unshakeable champion! Her passionate faith and selfless obedience were instrumental in making the gift of salvation available to every human being. And, rather like Jochebed's Moses, Mary's son would triumph over forces of evil.

Still, Mary's faith, along with that of the disciples, must have been greatly tested after Jesus' death. Their hopes and dreams for themselves and for the nation of Israel were completely ruined. They didn't entirely understand that God would raise Jesus from death—not even Mary knew. Yet after all the miraculous events surrounding God's purpose for Jesus were fully revealed, Mary would be present as the early church was born.

In my former book, Theophilus, I wrote about all that Jesus began to do and to teach until the day he was taken up to heaven, after giving instructions through the Holy Spirit to the apostles he had chosen. After his suffering, he presented himself to them and gave many convincing proofs that he was alive. He appeared to them over a period of forty days and spoke about the kingdom of God. On one occasion, while he was eating with them, he gave them this command: "Do not leave Jerusalem, but wait for the gift my Father promised, which you have heard me speak about. For John baptized with water, but in a few days you will be baptized with the Holy Spirit (Acts 1:1–5, NIV).

Then the apostles returned to Jerusalem from the hill called the Mount of Olives, a Sabbath day's walk from the city. When they arrived, they went upstairs to the room where they were staying. Those present were Peter, John, James and Andrew; Philip and Thomas, Bartholomew and Matthew; James son of Alphaeus and Simon the Zealot, and Judas son of James. They all joined together constantly in prayer, along with the women and Mary the mother of Jesus, and with his brothers (Acts 1:12–14, NIV).

In other words, God's plans are not always understandable to us. But we must stand *firm* in our faith as Mary did, and have trust in His tender mercy and unfailing love.

> *Are you willing to stand on God's promises*
> *as Mary did— even when you don't*
> *fully understand what He is doing?*

Chapter Sixteen

Woman, You Have Great Faith!"

And God is able to make all grace abound to you,
so that having all sufficiency in all things at all
times, you may abound in every good work.

—2 Corinthians 9:8 (ESV)

God's free pardon is the greatest miracle that anyone could ever receive. Yet it takes humility as well as faith to receive anything from God. The woman we're considering in this chapter embodies humility. She was a Canaanite, but had come to Jesus to beg for His help for her daughter. Her faith and meekness were so outstanding that she ended up being showcased by Jesus Himself.

> Leaving that place, Jesus withdrew to the region of Tyre and Sidon. A Canaanite woman from that vicinity came to him, crying out, "Lord, Son of David, have mercy on me! My daughter is demon-possessed and suffering terribly."

Jesus did not answer a word. So his disciples came to him and urged him, "Send her away, for she keeps crying out after us." He answered, "I was sent only to the lost sheep of Israel."

The woman came and knelt before him. "Lord, help me!" she said. He replied, "It is not right to take the children's bread and toss it to the dogs." "Yes it is, Lord," she said. "Even the dogs eat the crumbs that fall from their master's table."

Then Jesus said to her, "Woman, you have great faith! Your request is granted." And her daughter was healed at that moment (Matthew 15:21–28, NIV).

After reading this you might ask yourself why Jesus was initially so dismissive to this woman. His refusal and subsequent answers could even be misconstrued as racism, sexism, or some other form of bias. But a closer examination will reveal that His response had nothing at all to do with her being female or a Canaanite, but was instead the beginning of a lesson that Jesus knew He could draw from this remarkable woman's life.

We know from the Scriptures that Jesus was without prejudice. On at least one occasion He deliberately planned His journey so that He could speak with a Samaritan woman—and this at a time when both women and Samaritans were considered of low status by the Jews. (See John 4:1–42.)

It's also noteworthy that, when this encounter took place, Jesus was in Gentile territory and on a mission to Gentile people. He had ministered to Gentiles on many other occasions, even though the Jews generally considered Gentiles unworthy. Jesus however did not treat Gentiles as lesser people, so His words, "I was sent only to the lost sheep of Israel," do not negate the truth that God's message is for all.

> My dear children, I am writing this to you so that you will not sin. But if anyone does sin, we have an advocate who pleads our case before the Father. He is Jesus Christ, the one who is truly righteous. He himself is the sacrifice that atones for our sins—and not only our sins but the sins of all the world (1 John 2:1–2, NLT).

> For you are all children of God through faith in Christ Jesus. And all who have been united with Christ in baptism have put on Christ, like putting on new clothes. There is no longer Jew or Gentile, slave or free, male and female. For you are all one in Christ Jesus (Galatians 3:26–28, NLT).

Jesus, a master communicator who often spoke to the people through parables, was using the language of his time to say that the Jews were to be the first to have the opportunity to accept Him as Messiah, and that they would be the ones to spread the message of salvation to the rest of the world.

Believers in the God of Israel were often referred to as "sheep," so employing the metaphor "dogs" here was used to describe the spiritual condition of the Gentiles. They weren't a part of God's flock; instead they were "dogs," because they did not yet know God. According to Strong's Concordance, the word used here for dog was the Greek word *kunarion*, which can be translated as puppy, pet dog, or little dog. The analogy was more like that of a playful young daughter, sneaking food crumbs from the table for her puppy.

Jesus chose not to use the Greek word for wild dog's *kuōn*, which was, literally, a scavenging canine, and, figuratively, a spiritual predator who feeds off others. An example of this can be found in, "Do not give what is holy to dogs" (Matthew 7:6). Jesus' reference to the Canaanite woman as a "dog" was an image adapted from the people's own tongue in order to illustrate that it was not appropriate for sceptics (or "dogs") to have what only belonged to "sheep"—meaning those with faith.

By virtue of His divinity, Jesus knew that the woman's modest nature would shine through, even though she was a Gentile. She would prove that she was not a "dog" (or sceptic, as Gentiles were generally presumed to be) but a true believer in the God of Israel. Jesus was not in the business of being a stumbling block to anyone's faith! Instead, we're reminded in the Scriptures to continue "fixing our eyes on Jesus, the pioneer and perfecter of faith" (Hebrews 12:2, NIV).

This challenge was not designed to harm the woman or to prevent her from receiving a miracle for her daughter. Instead, it was a perfect opportunity to show the potential for Gentiles to demonstrate a still greater faith in God than some of God's own people. Gentiles would indeed be included in God's flock.

In His infinite wisdom, Jesus knew that the challenge would summon up the woman's faith, courage, and humility—that she would not be ensnared by pride, as so many people would have been. Instead, by demonstrating her own unshakeable faith, the Canaanite woman seized the opportunity given to her by God and received a miracle for her child. Although not yet a member of God's flock, her perseverance won the day.

What Jesus said to the woman sounds like an insult, but it was intentionally a challenge.

The woman rose to the challenge, just as Jesus knew she would, and revealed her outstanding humility. She was not fazed by His example of pet puppies, but instead reminded Him that His work would have a spillover effect and touch Gentiles as well as Jews. How apt!

For the LORD your God is God of Gods and Lord of lords, the great God, mighty and awesome, who shows no partiality and accepts no bribes (Deuteronomy 10:17, NIV).

Then Peter replied, "I see very clearly that God shows no favoritism. In every nation he accepts those who fear him and do what is right (Acts 10:34–35, NLT).

For God does not show favoritism (Romans 2:11, NLT).

Jesus was not called to change His assignment of reaching out first to the Jews, or to divert His limited earthly efforts toward the Gentiles or sceptics, but He gave this humble woman the miracle that she sought. "For this very reason, make every effort to add to your faith goodness; and to goodness, knowledge; and to knowledge, self-control; and to self-control, perseverance; and to perseverance, godliness" (2 Peter 1:5–6, NIV).

If confronted with a challenge from God, will you respond with humility and tenacity— or just give up and walk away?

Chapter Seventeen

NOT ENOUGH TO MORE THAN ENOUGH

*My help comes from the LORD, the
Maker of heaven and earth.*

—PSALM 121:2 (NIV)

When we respond to the negative circumstances in our own lives with unwavering faith, we will encounter God's abundance. This next example powerfully demonstrates that God wants to provide for and help us.

> When Jesus landed and saw a large crowd, he had compassion on them, because they were like sheep without a shepherd. So he began teaching them many things.
>
> By this time it was late in the day, so his disciples came to him. "This is a remote place," they said, "and it's already very late. Send the people away so that they can go to the surrounding

countryside and villages and buy themselves something to eat."

But he answered, "You give them something to eat."

They said to him, "That would take more than half a year's wages! Are we to go and spend that much on bread and give it to them to eat?"

"How many loaves do you have?" he asked. "Go and see."

When they found out, they said, "Five—and two fish."

Then Jesus directed them to have all the people sit down in groups on the green grass. So they sat down in groups of hundreds and fifties. Taking the five loaves and the two fish and looking up to heaven, he gave thanks and broke the loaves. Then he gave them to his disciples to distribute to the people. He also divided the two fish among them all. They all ate and were satisfied, and the disciples picked up twelve basketfuls of broken pieces of bread and fish. The number of the men who had eaten was five thousand (Mark 6:34–44, NIV).

Notice that, confronted with the need, Jesus' first action was to keep everyone in order by asking His disciples to organize those present into small groups. This is another key to obtaining God's help: when faced with seemingly insurmountable odds, don't focus on the problem and panic. Nothing useful can emerge from fear, panic, and disorderliness. Instead, initiate sensible actions toward solving the problem.

After settling everyone down, Jesus looked up to heaven and prayed. "I lift my eyes to you, O God, enthroned in heaven" (Psalm 123:1, NLT).

Show your gratitude for what you already possess, no matter how small it might be compared to the size of your need. This will open the doors to divine blessings.

"Enter his gates with thanksgiving and his courts with praise; give thanks to him and praise his name" (Psalm 100:4, NIV). Although Jesus was expected to meet this sizable responsibility with nothing but a few loaves of bread and two fish, He didn't grumble or complain. He first thanked God for what He already had, even though it must have been obvious that five loaves and two fish could never satisfy such a large crowd. Some members of his audience probably thought that he was joking. Yet Jesus knew that God would do the impossible, out of His great love.

Giving thanks to God for what we already possess creates an atmosphere where not enough can become *more than enough*. Regardless of any pressures that we may face, we must remember that the miraculous blessings that God has in store will not manifest themselves in our lives without unwavering trust in Him. "But when you ask, you must believe and not doubt, because the one who doubts is like a wave of the sea, blown and tossed by the wind. That person should not expect to receive anything from the Lord. Such a person is double-minded and unstable in all they do (James 1:6–8, NIV).

We also learned, from Jochebed, that the right direction, whenever we're seeking anything from God, is forward. So create momentum by taking whatever action you can to move your situation forward; this positions you to receive God's blessings.

> *Don't allow doubts or fears to prevent you*
> *from experiencing the rich and satisfying life*
> *that God has in mind for every one of us!*

After the miracle had taken place and the people had eaten until they were full, the crumbs that were left over and gathered by the disciples were enough to fill twelve baskets! Truly, life in all its abundance! "If you are willing and obedient, you will eat the good things of the land" (Isaiah 1:19, NIV).

> *Our Creator is ready, willing and able to*
> *take care of all of our needs. Are you willing*
> *to place your complete trust in Him?*

Chapter Eighteen

"RAISE THE ROOF" FAITH!

As iron sharpens iron, so a friend
sharpens a friend.

—PROVERBS 27:17 (NLT)

The Collins English Dictionary describes "raise the roof" as "create a boisterous disturbance." And this was exactly what four awesome people did for their paralyzed friend as he lay helpless on his bed. This man's loyal, determined, and gutsy friends decided to assist someone no longer in a position to fight the good fight by himself. Their efforts remind us that the company we keep greatly impacts our lives.

> *We need to choose our friends wisely. We should*
> *never deceive ourselves about the nature of the*
> *people with whom we choose to surround ourselves.*

Our relationships can be critical to the outcomes of our lives and—make no mistake—we are personally responsible for the company that we keep. "Do not be misled: 'Bad company corrupts good character'" (1 Corinthians 15:33, NIV).

These four friends were so determined to save their sick comrade that they were willing to go the extra mile to get him the help he needed. So great was their faith that the foremost thought in their minds was getting their loved one into the presence of Jesus.

> Jesus could no longer openly enter a town, but was out in desolate places, and people were coming to him from every quarter (Mark 1:45, ESV).

> And when he returned to Capernaum after some days, it was reported that he was at home. And many were gathered together, so that there was no more room, not even at the door. And he was preaching the word to them. And they came, bringing to him a paralytic carried by four men. And when they could not get near him because of the crowd, they removed the roof above him, and when they had made an opening, they let down the bed on which the paralytic lay. And when Jesus saw their faith,

he said to the paralytic, "Son, your sins are forgiven (Mark 2:1–5, ESV).

But that you may know that the Son of Man
has authority on earth to forgive sins," he said
to the paralytic—"I say to you, rise, pick up your
bed, and go home." And he rose and immediately picked up his bed and went out before
them all, so that they were all amazed and glorified God, saying, "We never saw anything like
this!" (Mark 2:10–12, ESV).

Cutting a hole in a roof large enough to get a bed
through is a pretty big task, yet nothing deterred the
four heroes. They were willing to try anything to ensure
that their friend did not miss this once-in-a-lifetime
opportunity to experience an encounter with God.
What a ruckus must have happened as the gang of four
tore off the roof and triumphantly lowered their friend
to where Jesus stood. Their faith spoke so powerfully
to Jesus that He couldn't help but take notice. So Jesus
interrupted Himself, stopped preaching, and quietly
healed the paralytic man.

A mother's love is practically deified in many cul-
tures. But I doubt that even the most devoted parent
could have surpassed these four friends in the strength
of their love. I also can't help wondering what sort of

friend the paralytic man must have been to them, to make them willing to go to such lengths. The friends also demonstrated that, whenever Jesus was around, a miracle was always possible. Because "with God all things are possible" (Matthew 19:26, NIV).

> *It bears repeating that it's crucial to choose friends wisely. Surround yourself with loving, faith-filled companions; they may well play significant roles in your life.*

Being part of a healthy, Christ-centered, faith community also contributes greatly to spiritual growth, in addition to being a great place to meet like-minded people whose love, support, and prayers can be indispensable during difficult times. Our lives were not designed to be lived in isolation: we all need each other. When your burdens become too heavy to bear on your own, let friends share some of your burdens.

"Share each other's burdens, and in this way obey the law of Christ" (Galatians 6:2, NLT).

Two people are better off than one, for they can help each other succeed. If one person falls, the other can reach out and help. But someone who falls alone is in real trouble. Likewise, two people lying close together can keep each other warm.

But how can one be warm alone? A person standing alone can be attacked and defeated, but two can stand back-to-back and conquer. Three are even better, for a triple-braided cord is not easily broken (Ecclesiastes 4:9–12, NLT).

Ask yourself the following questions to assess what type of friends you currently have. If your answers to both questions below are no, you may want to find yourself some new loving and faithful friends—or be more responsive to the type of friend you are to others.

Am I the kind of friend that others can rely on?
If I were suddenly unable to care for myself, would
my friends be willing to help me the way that
the paralyzed man's friends helped him?

Blind Bartimaeus

Another person who caused a boisterous disturbance in order to receive a miracle from Jesus was a blind man by the name of Bartimaeus, who had been reduced to begging in order to survive. He had been blind so long that people even identified him by his condition, branding him "blind Bartimaeus." But when he heard that Jesus was around, Bartimaeus chose to unleash his faith. A miracle was within his grasp and he was determined to possess it.

Then they reached Jericho, and as Jesus and his disciples left town, a large crowd followed him. A blind beggar named Bartimaeus (son of Timaeus) was sitting beside the road. When Bartimaeus heard that Jesus of Nazareth was nearby, he began to shout, "Jesus, Son of David, have mercy on me!"

"Be quiet!" many of the people yelled at him.

But he only shouted louder, "Son of David, have mercy on me!"

When Jesus heard him, he stopped and said, "Tell him to come here."

So they called the blind man. "Cheer up," they said. "Come on, he's calling you!"

Bartimaeus threw aside his coat, jumped up, and came to Jesus

"What do you want me to do for you?" Jesus asked.

"My Rabbi," the blind man said, "I want to see!"

And Jesus said to him, "Go, for your faith has healed you." Instantly the man could see, and he followed Jesus down the road (Mark 10:46–52, NLT).

Isn't it interesting that the same people who yelled at Bartimaeus to be quiet ended up cheering him on? Because they themselves could see, they had failed to empathize with his plight. *Sometimes, people fail to have compassion for others when they are not personally affected.* But Bartimaeus was so desperate that he only shouted louder. He gained Jesus' attention and taught all of us that "raising the roof" faith isn't about submitting to social norms or allowing others to dictate what happens to us. Instead, it's about giving our all in our times of trial.

Don't allow others to determine how or if you'll receive help from God. Press on regardless, fighting the good fight of faith. When your unshakeable faith connects with God's power, awesome things can happen!

Are you as determined as Bartimaeus
to receive your answer from God?

Chapter Nineteen

THE CENTURION AND ABRAHAM'S GOBSMACKING FAITH

It is written: "I believed; therefore I have spoken." Since we have that same spirit of faith, we also believe and therefore speak.

—2 CORINTHIANS 4:13 (NIV)

God works in ways that far surpass anything that human beings can manage on their own, but first we have to believe in His word. If we choose to keep our doubts and fears alive by feeding on skepticism instead of the daily nourishment of Scripture, we might be robbed of some awesome answers to prayers. As we begin to approach the end of our discussion, I was reminded of this in the account of the life of a man simply described by Luke as "the centurion"—someone who demonstrated such impressive faith that he even amazed Jesus!

When Jesus had finished saying all this to the people who were listening, he entered Capernaum. There a centurion's servant, whom his master valued highly, was sick and about to die. The centurion heard of Jesus and sent some elders of the Jews to him, asking him to come and heal his servant. When they came to Jesus, they pleaded earnestly with him, "This man deserves to have you do this, because he loves our nation and has built our synagogue." So Jesus went with them.

He was not far from the house when the centurion sent friends to say to him: "Lord, don't trouble yourself, for I do not deserve to have you come under my roof. That is why I did not even consider myself worthy to come to you. But say the word, and my servant will be healed. For I myself am a man under authority, with soldiers under me. I tell this one, 'Go,' and he goes; and that one, 'Come,' and he comes. I say to my servant, 'Do this,' and he does it."

When Jesus heard this, he was amazed at him, and turning to the crowd following him, he said, "I tell you, I have not found such great faith even in Israel." Then the men who had been sent returned to the house and found the servant well (Luke 7:1–10, NIV).

Wow! Just as with the Canaanite woman, here was a person not yet belonging to God's covenant, but still displaying far more faith in God than His own people.

This proves that God doesn't play favorites; anyone can choose to have faith and thus open him- or herself to God's abundance.

> *The centurion honored God by displaying*
> *a childlike trust and faith in Him. We all*
> *ought to come to God as humble, obedient*
> *children, not distrustful, defiant ones.*

Living on a planet where emphasis is constantly placed on things that we can see, touch, feel, or even scientifically prove makes it harder for us to believe in God. But although we cannot "see" Him, He proves His existence and power millions of times each day, simply through His creation.

> For since the creation of the world, God's invisible qualities—his eternal power and divine nature—have been clearly seen, being understood from what has been made, so that people are without excuse (Romans 1: 20, NIV).

> Yes, they knew God, but they wouldn't worship him as God or even give him thanks. And they began to think up foolish ideas of what God was like. As a result, their minds became dark and confused (Romans 1:21, NLT).

Just as a painting is the evidence of the existence of a painter, all of creation overflows with evidence that points toward the creator. God delights in rewarding those who place their trust in Him, as the anonymous centurion did. God's word is all we need.

Is His word good with you?

Abraham

No discussion about faith would be complete without mentioning the man sometimes called "the great father of faith," Abraham. His devotion to God was legendary. In some ways, he left us the most patient example of faith to follow. (Also, notice in the following account that it was the word of God that first came to Abraham, inspiring faith in his heart.)

> *The word of the Lord came to Abram in a vision*: "Do not be afraid, Abram. I am your shield, your very great reward."
>
> But Abram said, "Sovereign Lord, what can you give me since I remain childless and the one who will inherit my estate is Eliezer of Damascus?" And Abram said, "You have given me no children; so a servant in my household will be my heir."
>
> *Then the word of the Lord came to him*: "This man will not be your heir, but a son who is your own

flesh and blood will be your heir." He took him outside and said, "Look up at the sky and count the stars—if indeed you can count them." Then he said to him, "So shall your offspring be."

Abram believed the Lord, and he credited it to him as righteousness.

He also said to him, "I am the Lord, who brought you out of Ur of the Chaldeans to give you this land to take possession of it."

But Abram said, "Sovereign Lord, how can I know that I will gain possession of it?"

So the Lord said to him, "Bring me a heifer, a goat and a ram, each three years old, along with a dove and a young pigeon."

Abram brought all these to him, cut them in two and arranged the halves opposite each other; the birds, however, he did not cut in half. Then birds of prey came down on the carcasses, but Abram drove them away.

As the sun was setting, Abram fell into a deep sleep, and a thick and dreadful darkness came over him (Genesis 15:1–12, NIV; emphasis added).

When the sun had set and darkness had fallen, a smoking firepot with a blazing torch appeared and passed between the pieces. On that day the Lord made a covenant with Abram and said, "To your descendants I give this land, from the Wadi of Egypt to the great river, the Euphrates—the land of the Kenites, Kenizzites, Kadmonites, Hittites, Perizzites, Rephaites, Amorites, Canaanites, Girgashites and Jebusites" (Genesis 15:17–21, NIV).

Then the Lord said to him, "Know for certain that for four hundred years your descendants will be strangers in a country not their own and that they will be enslaved and mistreated there. But I will punish the nation they serve as slaves, and afterward they will come out with great possessions. You, however, will go to your ancestors in peace and be buried at a good old age. In the fourth generation your descendants will come back here, for the sin of the Amorites has not yet reached its full measure" (Genesis 15:13–16, NIV).

When Abram was ninety-nine years old, the Lord appeared to him and said, "I am God Almighty; walk before me faithfully and be blameless. Then I will make my covenant between me and you and will greatly increase your numbers." Abram fell facedown, and God said to him, "As for me, this is my covenant with you: You will be the father of many nations. No longer will you be called Abram; your name will be Abraham, for I have made you a father of many nations. I will make you very fruitful; I will make nations of you, and kings will come from you. I will establish my covenant as an everlasting covenant between me and you and your descendants after you for the generations to come, to be your God and the God of your descendants after you. The whole land of Canaan, where you now reside as a foreigner, I will give as an everlasting possession to you and your descendants after you; and I will be their God (Genesis 17:1–8, NIV).

God also said to Abraham, "As for Sarai your wife, you are no longer to call her Sarai; her name will be Sarah. I will bless her and will surely give you a son by her. I will bless her so that she will be the mother of nations; kings of peoples will come from her."

Abraham fell facedown; he laughed and said to himself, "Will a son be born to a man a hundred years old? Will Sarah bear a child at the age of ninety?" (Genesis 17:15–17, NIV).

Now the Lord was gracious to Sarah as he had said, and the Lord did for Sarah what he had promised. Sarah became pregnant and bore a son to Abraham in his old age, at the very time God had promised him. Abraham gave the name Isaac to the son Sarah bore him (Genesis 21:1–3, NIV).

Abraham was a hundred years old when his son Isaac was born to him. Sarah said, "God has brought me laughter, and everyone who hears about this will laugh with me."

And she added, "Who would have said to Abraham that Sarah would nurse children? Yet I have borne him a son in his old age" (Genesis 21:5–7, NIV).

Abraham personified patient and limitless faith. He implicitly believed in God's promises, regardless of how long he had to anticipate their fulfillment. And even when Abraham found what God was promising almost laughable, he still displayed unshakeable faith.

Unbelief is often the root cause of shaky faith. Abraham's faith never wavered, despite having to wait a very long time to receive what God had promised.

Abraham chose to continue to believe in God's promise, because he was fully convinced that God would bring to pass what He had promised.

So the promise is received by faith. It is given as a free gift. And we are all certain to receive it, whether or not we live according to the Law of Moses, if we have faith like Abraham's. For Abraham is the father of all who believe. That is what the Scriptures mean when God told him, "I have made you the father of many nations." This happened because Abraham believed in the God who brings the dead back to life and who creates new things out of nothing.

Even when there was no reason for hope, Abraham kept hoping—believing that he would become the father of many nations. For God had said to him, "That's how many descendants you will have!" And Abraham's faith did not weaken even though, at about one hundred years of age, he figured his body was as good as dead—and so was Sarah's womb.

Abraham never wavered in believing God's promise. In fact, his faith grew stronger, and in this he brought glory to God. He was fully convinced that God is able to do whatever he promises. And because of Abraham's faith, God counted him as righteous. And when God counted him as righteous, it wasn't just for Abraham's benefit. It was recorded for our benefit too, assuring us that God will also count us as righteous if we believe in him, the one who raised Jesus our Lord from the dead. He was handed over to die because of our sins, and he was raised to life to make us right with God (Romans 4:16–25, NLT).

It must have seemed like an excruciating wait for Abraham before God's promise was finally fulfilled. He was one hundred years old when his wife Sarah finally gave birth to their son Isaac, whose name by the way means laughter. We must endeavor to hold on to God's promises and demonstrate our unshakeable faith in Him *even when the wait is longer than we ever imagined.*

We do not want you to become lazy, but to imitate those who through faith and patience inherit what has been promised. When God made his promise to Abraham, since there was no one greater for him to swear by, he swore by himself, saying, "I will surely bless you and give you many descendants." And so after waiting patiently, Abraham received what was promised (Hebrews 6:12–15, NIV).

The son that God eventually blessed Abraham and Sarah with, Isaac, grew up to be one of the founding fathers of the nation of Israel. And, yes, the descendants of Abraham were far too numerous to count, all because one man held onto God's word. And as can also be learnt from the Israelites—Abraham's descendants—our parents' faith, like our grandparents' or great-grandparents', will not automatically be transferred to us. The Israelites did not exercise the same type of unshakeable trust in God that their forefather Abraham had. They instead chose not to believe, but murmured and complained against Him on many occasions.

We are each individually responsible for our own decisions about faith. Once the message of God's free pardon through Jesus Christ has been shared with us, we have the free choice whether or not to accept God's offer of forgiveness for our sins. But if we say "Yes!" to God, according to Scripture, something amazing happens: "Now that you belong to Christ, you are the true children of Abraham. You are his heirs, and God's promise to Abraham belongs to you (Galatians 3:29, NLT).

If you wait patiently for God, God will never fail you.

Will you choose to have unshakeable faith in God, regardless of how long it might take before you can realize the fulfillment of His promise?

Chapter Twenty

FAITH AFTER FAILURE

*He forgives all my sins and
heals all my diseases.*

—PSALM 103:3 (NLT)

Recovering from a major setback or serious failure can sometimes feel overwhelming; the crushing disappointment can be very hard to bear. Without God's help, we may feel utterly unable to move forward from perceived defeat to the light and radiance of God's forgiveness on the other side. Faith and courage are needed to overcome our biggest failures. Some important lessons can be drawn from the lives of two other Bible heroes, the Apostle Peter and King David of Israel.

To start with Peter, he was, of course, one of the very first disciples handpicked by Jesus and went on to become one of His most trusted followers (see Luke 5:1–11). The only disciple to walk on water (see Matthew 14:22–29), Peter also wrote two books of the Bible, having left his family, his fishing business, and the rest of his life behind in order to follow Jesus. Peter also witnessed more than one occasion when Jesus raised the dead (see John 11, Luke 8:40–56, and Luke 7:11–17).

But after following Jesus for almost three years, Peter's life proved that any of us, even the most devout and faithful, can fail, should we become careless. It's vital on our journey of faith never to become overconfident. Instead, we must constantly humble ourselves before God.

> *None of us—not even Jesus' leading disciples—*
> *are immune from sinning against God. We must*
> *always remain humble, watchful, and prayerful.*

Then Jesus told them,

"This very night you will all fall away on account of me, for it is written: 'I will strike the shepherd, and the sheep of the flock will be scattered.'

"But after I have risen, I will go ahead of you into Galilee."

Peter replied, "Even if all fall away on account of you, I never will."

"Truly I tell you," Jesus answered, "this very night, before the rooster crows, you will disown me three times." But Peter declared, "Even if I have to die with you, I will never disown you."

And all the other disciples said the same (Matthew 26:31–35, NIV).

A crowd approached, led by Judas, one of the twelve disciples. Judas walked over to Jesus to greet him with a kiss. But Jesus said, "Judas, would you betray the Son of Man with a kiss?" (Luke 22:47–48, NLT).

So they arrested him and led him to the high priest's home. And Peter followed at a distance. The guards lit a fire in the middle of the courtyard and sat around it, and Peter joined them there. A servant girl noticed him in the firelight and began staring at him. Finally she said,

"This man was one of Jesus' followers!"

But Peter denied it. "Woman," he said, "I don't even know him!"

After a while someone else looked at him and said, "You must be one of them!"

"No, man, I'm not!" Peter retorted.

About an hour later someone else insisted, *"This must be one of them, because he is a Galilean, too."*

But Peter said,

"Man, I don't know what you are talking about." And immediately, while he was still speaking, the rooster crowed.

At that moment the Lord turned and looked at Peter. Suddenly, the Lord's words flashed through Peter's mind: "Before the rooster crows tomorrow morning, you will deny three times that you even know me." And Peter left the courtyard, weeping bitterly (Luke 22:54–62, NLT; emphasis added).

The waves of persecution against Jesus and His followers were already strong and getting stronger when Peter made his solemn vow never to betray his friend. The chances of getting beaten, thrown into prison, or killed were already high, yet Peter still chose to make this pledge to his Lord—wildly overestimating his own loyalty and courage.

One of the most damaging hurts
of all is the act of betrayal.

This is because it arises from those to whom we are close and, generally, from those from whom we least expect it. After his betrayal of Jesus, Peter found it hard to recover from his sense of failure and humiliation, so he abandoned His call from God and returned to fishing.

Simon Peter said, "I'm going fishing.
"We'll come, too," they all said. So they

went out in the boat, but they caught nothing all night.

At dawn Jesus was standing on the beach, but the disciples couldn't see who he was. He called out, "Fellows, have you caught any fish?"

"No," they replied.

Then he said, "Throw out your net on the right-hand side of the boat, and you'll get some!"

So they did, and they couldn't haul in the net because there were so many fish in it.

Then the disciple Jesus loved said to Peter, "It's the Lord!" When Simon Peter heard that it was the Lord, he put on his tunic (for he had stripped for work), jumped into the water, and headed to shore. The others stayed with the boat and pulled the loaded net to the shore, for they were only about a hundred yards from shore. When they got there, they found breakfast waiting for them—fish cooking over a charcoal fire, and some bread.

"Bring some of the fish you've just caught," Jesus said. So Simon Peter went aboard and dragged the net to the shore. There were 153 large fish, and yet the net hadn't torn. "Now come and have some breakfast!" Jesus said.

None of the disciples dared to ask him, "Who are you?" They knew it was the Lord.

Then Jesus served them the bread and the fish. This was the third time Jesus had appeared to his disciples since he had been raised from the dead. After breakfast Jesus asked Simon Peter, "Simon son of John, do you love me more than these?"

"Yes, Lord," Peter replied, "you know I love you."

"Then feed my lambs," Jesus told him. Jesus repeated the question: "Simon son of John, do you love me?"

"Yes, Lord," Peter said, "you know I love you."

"Then take care of my sheep," Jesus said. A third time he asked him, "Simon son of John, do you love me?"

Peter was hurt that Jesus asked the question a third time. He said, "Lord, you know everything. You know that I love you." Jesus said, "Then feed my sheep." . . . Then Jesus told him, "Follow me." (John 21:3–17, 19, NLT).

Peter's recovery of heart and nerve after betraying Jesus required divine intervention, as well as genuine repentance. He had denied knowing Him three times, but would be given a fresh opportunity to reaffirm his love for Jesus again the same number of times. We need to offer the same repentance toward anyone whom we might have offended or, still worse, betrayed.

God showed His own infinite mercy and grace by fully forgiving and restoring Peter. (But we already knew that God's grace has no measure! Did he not send Jesus?) After Peter had abandoned his first ministry, Jesus interceded and restored him to his eminence amongst all His disciples. Where would we all have been had Peter permanently given up ministry for fishing nets? The countless souls won to God by Peter's dedication, passion, and power might never even have heard the Gospel! But God's grace proved far stronger than human sin and failure.

> *Failing doesn't make us failures—unless*
> *we choose to remain in that state.*

In other words, don't allow yourself to remain in a defeated state! Instead, allow your sorrow to birth a new humility and a still greater appreciation for God's grace and mercy. And then extend the same grace that you have received to others.

> *It takes humility and faith to face God again*
> *after we have failed Him, a process that*
> *begins with receiving His forgiveness and*
> *ends by being able to forgive ourselves.*

Through this we receive the compassion and wisdom that will help us to assist others when they fail.

Praise be to the God and Father of our Lord Jesus Christ, the Father of compassion and the God of all comfort, who comforts us in all our troubles, so that we can comfort those in any trouble with the comfort we ourselves receive from God (2 Corinthians 1:3–4, NIV).

Where sin increased, grace increased all the more (Romans 5:20, NIV).

So just as sin ruled over all people and brought them to death, now God's wonderful grace rules instead, giving us right standing with God and resulting in eternal life through Jesus Christ our Lord (Romans 5:21, NLT).

Will you genuinely repent of your past failures and gratefully receive God's pardon? Can you find it in your heart to move on?

King David's Scandal

"Flee the evil desires of youth" (2 Timothy 2:22, NIV). I shared a great deal about King David of Israel in a previous book (*Giving God Ultimate Love: Over-the-Top Mega Love*). David was a passionate believer: he once danced before God with such enthusiasm that he was insulted by his wife (see 2 Samuel 6:14–22). His devotion to God played a huge role in how he led the nation, and he also composed many stirring and beautiful psalms. In short, the behavior King David exhibits below was not typical. Instead, this story provides strong reinforcement of the truth that we're never too big or important to fail.

> In the spring, at the time when kings go off to war, David sent Joab out with the king's men and the whole Israelite army. They destroyed the Ammonites and besieged Rabbah. But David remained in Jerusalem.
>
> One evening David got up from his bed and walked around on the roof of the palace. From the roof he saw a woman bathing. The woman was very beautiful, and David sent someone to find out about her. The man said, "She is Bathsheba, the daughter of Eliam and the wife of Uriah the Hittite." Then David sent messengers to get her. She came to him, and he slept with her. (Now she was purifying herself from her monthly uncleanness.) Then she went back home. The woman conceived and sent word to David, saying, "I am pregnant."
>
> So David sent this word to Joab: "Send me Uriah the Hittite." And Joab sent him to David. When Uriah came to him, David asked him how Joab was, how the soldiers were, and how

the war was going. Then David said to Uriah, "Go down to your house and wash your feet." So Uriah left the palace, and a gift from the king was sent after him. But Uriah slept at the entrance to the palace with all his master's servants and did not go down to his house.

David was told, "Uriah did not go home." So he asked Uriah, "Haven't you just come from a military campaign? Why didn't you go home?"

Uriah said to David, "The ark and Israel and Judah are staying in tents, and my commander Joab and my lord's men are camped in the open country. How could I go to my house to eat and drink and make love to my wife? As surely as you live, I will not do such a thing!"

Then David said to him, "Stay here one more day, and tomorrow I will send you back." So Uriah remained in Jerusalem that day and the next. At David's invitation, he ate and drank with him, and David made him drunk. But in the evening Uriah went out to sleep on his mat among his master's servants; he did not go home.

In the morning David wrote a letter to Joab and sent it with Uriah. In it he wrote, "Put Uriah out in front where the fighting is fiercest. Then withdraw from him so he will be struck down and die."

So while Joab had the city under siege, he put Uriah at a place where he knew the strongest defenders were. When the men of the city came out and fought against Joab, some of the men in David's army fell; moreover, Uriah the Hittite died.

Joab sent David a full account of the battle. He instructed the messenger: "When you have finished giving the king this account of the battle, the king's anger may flare up, and he may ask you, 'Why did you get so close to the city to fight? Didn't you know they would shoot arrows from the wall? Who killed Abimelek son of Jerub-Besheth? Didn't a woman drop an upper millstone on him from the wall, so that he died in Thebez? Why did you get so close to the wall?' If he asks you this, then say to him, 'Moreover, your servant Uriah the Hittite is dead.'"

The messenger set out, and when he arrived he told David everything Joab had sent him to say. The messenger said to David, "The men overpowered us and came out against us in the open, but we drove them back to the entrance of the city gate. Then the archers shot arrows at your servants from the wall, and some of the king's men died. Moreover, your servant Uriah the Hittite is dead."

David told the messenger, "Say this to Joab: 'Don't let this upset you; the sword devours one as well as another. Press the attack against the city and destroy it.' Say this to encourage Joab."

When Uriah's wife heard that her husband was dead, she mourned for him. After the time of mourning was over, David had her brought to his house, and she became his wife and bore him a son. But the thing David had done displeased the Lord (2 Samuel 11, NIV).

Here we have a man who loved the Lord and had been greatly favored by Him—yet still he failed! Had David stayed strongly connected to God, it could all have been so different. The message is that we need to be vigilant and prayerful so that, even after attaining our highest goals, we won't fall into abject disgrace.

Never let your love for God grow cold!

Because of the increase of wickedness, the love of most will grow cold, but the one who stands firm to the end will be saved (Matthew 24:12–13, NIV).

But each person is tempted when they are dragged away by their own evil desire and enticed. Then, after desire has conceived, it gives birth to sin; and sin, when it is full-grown, gives birth to death (James 1:14–15, NIV).

The choices David made almost led to his irretrievable downfall. And it all began with his being at the wrong place at the wrong time. At a time when kings usually go out to war, David was relaxing at home, because he had been blessed with peace in his territory by God and had become lazy. He no longer felt the need to go out to watchfully defend or expand his territory. And he'd not only lost his cutting edge as a warrior, he had probably also stopped the spiritual practices that had first brought him to power—because it's hard to fall into sin while fervently following God.

Instead, David schemed to possess something—another man's wife—not rightfully his. And in his attempt to cover up his adultery, he committed the still more horrific crime of murder. At heart, David had stopped being spiritually vigilant. This led him to give way to lust and even to murder, despite the fact that he already had several wives of his own (incidentally, another behavior prohibited by God).

Be sure to appoint over you a king the Lord your God chooses. He must be from among your fellow Israelites. Do not place a foreigner over you, one who is not an Israelite. The king, moreover, must not acquire great numbers of horses for himself or

make the people return to Egypt to get more of
them, for the Lord has told you, "You are not to
go back that way again." He must not take many
wives, or his heart will be led astray (Deuteronomy
17:15–17, NIV).

Yet who can intercede for us when the person whom
we have offended is God Himself? As we learned from
Peter's personal challenges, it can be very hard to recover
after falling from God's grace. Letting down the people
whom we love, and bringing notoriety upon ourselves
and our families, can lead to indescribable depths of
regret, sorrow, and shame.

> *Prideful behavior—including overestimating*
> *our ability to stay true to God—can prove*
> *spiritually dangerous.*
> *Whatever it took to obtain what you have*
> *is what it will take to maintain it.*

Also, others may still doubt us, even after we have
repented. It takes unshakeable faith to sorrowfully
restore our broken connections with God and to attempt
to regain all the trust that we've lost. This can only be
accomplished by casting ourselves on God's grace. Of
course, we need God's grace in every way, but especially
when recovering from mistakes.

*Submitting ourselves to God with humility
and genuine repentance is the only way to
successfully resist or overcome evil.*

Abiding faithfully in God's word and staying obedient to Him is God's definition of love. "If you love me, you will keep my commandments" (John 14:15, ESV).

When King David finally stopped deceiving himself, he showed us the way back to God when he penned the following unforgettable prayer of repentance:

Have mercy on me, O God,
   because of your unfailing love.
Because of your great compassion,
   blot out the stain of my sins.
Wash me clean from my guilt.
   Purify me from my sin.
For I recognize my rebellion;
   it haunts me day and night.
Against you, and you alone, have I sinned;
   I have done what is evil in your sight.
You will be proved right in what you say,
   and your judgment against me is just.
For I was born a sinner—
   yes, from the moment my mother conceived me.
But you desire honesty from the womb,
   teaching me wisdom even there.

Purify me from my sins, and I will be clean;
   wash me, and I will be whiter than snow.
Oh, give me back my joy again;
   you have broken me—
   now let me rejoice.
   Don't keep looking at my sins.
Remove the stain of my guilt.
   Create in me a clean heart, O God.
Renew a loyal spirit within me.
   Do not banish me from your presence,
   and don't take your Holy Spirit from me.
Restore to me the joy of your salvation,
   and make me willing to obey you.
Then I will teach your ways to rebels,
   and they will return to you.
Forgive me for shedding blood, O God who
   saves;
   then I will joyfully sing of Your forgiveness.
Unseal my lips, O Lord,
   that my mouth may praise you.
You do not desire a sacrifice, or I would offer
   one.
   You do not want a burnt offering.
The sacrifice you desire is a broken spirit.
   You will not reject a broken and repentant
   heart, O God.

Look with favor on Zion and help her;
   rebuild the walls of Jerusalem.
Then you will be pleased with sacrifices
   offered in the right spirit—
   with burnt offerings and whole burnt
   offerings.
Then bulls will again be sacrificed on your
   altar
(Psalm 51, NLT)

In the Old Testament, as we know, the punishment for adultery was death.

If a man commits adultery with another man's wife—with the wife of his neighbor—both the adulterer and the adulteress are to be put to death (Leviticus 20:10, NIV).

But after David's full and feeling repentance, God forgave him and even allowed him to continue as Israel's leader.

Then David confessed to Nathan, "I have sinned against the LORD."
   "Nathan replied, "Yes, but the LORD has forgiven you, and you won't die for this sin" (2 Samuel 12:13, NLT).

Just as He had with Peter, God fully restored David to the position and the purpose that He had always intended for him.

> "God opposes the proud but gives grace to the humble. So humble yourselves before God. Resist the devil, and he will flee from you. Come close to God, and God will come close to you. Wash your hands, you sinners; purify your hearts" (James 4:6–8, NLT).

We're able to appreciate God's grace far more deeply after our failures than we did before them.

The lesson here is that we should make every effort to put right each of the relationships that we have destroyed by our failures, starting with our relationship with God. We need to do this by taking complete ownership of our own wrongdoing. God will completely pardon us when we genuinely repent; God wipes our slate completely clean. (An example: the first son born to David by Bathsheba died. But God gave David another son, named Solomon, who inherited David's throne and shed glory on his name.)

King Solomon is recorded in the Bible as being one of the wisest and wealthiest kings who ever lived. God's blessing Solomon to this extent shows us the completeness of God's forgiveness. He also showed His grace and mercy toward David even more when His only begotten son Jesus Christ the savior of the whole world, was listed among David's direct descendants.

"For the Scriptures clearly state that the Messiah will be born of the royal line of David, in Bethlehem, the village where King David was born." John 7:42 (NLT).

Have you ever been involved in a scandal?
Are you willing to repent and receive God's
grace to overcome it?
Are you willing to offer the same forgiveness to others?

Chapter Twenty-One

STRENGTH FOR TODAY AND BRIGHT HOPE FOR TOMORROW

The godly may trip seven times,
but they will get up again.

—PROVERBS 24:16 (NLT)

fter thinking about God's grace toward King David of Israel and the Apostle Peter, some words from a popular Christian hymn, "Great is Thy Faithfulness," sprang to my mind. They were written by Thomas Chisholm, an American pastor from Kentucky, and assure us of God's faithfulness throughout every season of our lives.

> Great is thy faithfulness, O God my Father;
> There is no shadow of turning with thee;
> Thou changest not, thy compassions, they fail not;
> As thou hast been thou forever wilt be.
> Great is thy faithfulness!
> Great is thy faithfulness!

Morning by morning new mercies I see:
All I have needed thy hand hath provided—
Great is thy faithfulness, Lord, unto me!
Pardon for sin and a peace that endureth
Thine own dear presence to cheer and to guide;
Strength for today and bright hope for tomorrow
Blessings all mine, with ten thousand beside.

Our sense of gratitude to God, like our spiritual
strength, needs daily replenishment.

In order to be spiritually strong, and empowered by His grace, we need God's word every day, just as we nourish our bodies with nutritious food. This, accompanied by worship and prayers—as in Daniel's example—strengthens us to endure and overcome any adversity we might encounter. "Joyful are those who have the God of Israel as their helper, whose hope is in the LORD their God" (Psalm 146:5, NLT).

Of course, Jesus, Jochebed, the Shunammite woman, and many other faith heroes in our examples similarly faced insurmountable odds—yet each displayed that spiritual strength that is God's gift to believers under unimaginable pressures. "And this same God who takes care of me will supply all your needs from his glorious riches, which have been given to us in Christ Jesus" (Philippians 4:19, NLT).

As millions of people on our planet are suddenly faced with seemingly impossible situations, we must encourage each other never to give up and to pray daily for fresh strength from God. Even when we're at our weakest, God's strength is enough to carry us through!

> Search for the LORD and for his strength; continually seek him (Psalm 105:4, NLT).

> Let the weak say, I am strong (Joel 3:10, KJV 2000).

> Say to the people, "This is what the LORD says: 'When people fall down, don't they get up again?'" (Jeremiah 8:4, NLT).

Amidst the many powerful pressures being experienced across the planet, we have the opportunity to sift through the debris of our own pasts and to rebuild our lives on the rock-solid foundation that is God.

> The LORD is my rock, my fortress, and my savior; my God is my rock, in whom I find protection. He is my shield, the power that saves me, and my place of safety (Psalm 18:2, NLT).

> Therefore everyone who hears these words of mine and puts them into practice is like a wise

man who built his house on the rock. The rain came down, the streams rose, and the winds blew and beat against that house; yet it did not fall, because it had its foundation on the rock. But everyone who hears these words of mine and does not put them into practice is like a foolish man who built his house on sand. The rain came down, the streams rose, and the winds blew and beat against that house, and it fell with a great crash (Matthew 7:24–27, NIV).

It was not the rain, the wind, or the floods that brought the second of the two houses down, but its weak foundations. May your "faith house" be built on rock!

Many believe that Christians have been called to live extraordinary lives and do extraordinary things. But we've *all* actually been called to make known our extraordinary God.

Revealing the one who lives in us by faith—Jesus Christ—and yielding to God in an age of defiance toward Him brings glory to God.

Therefore, exercise your own unshakeable faith in God. The more faith that we have and exercise, the more pleasure we bring to our Creator. "You are worthy, O Lord, to receive glory and honor and power: for you have created all things, and for your pleasure they are and were created" (Revelation 4:11, KJV 2000).

> *Remember: When the impulsive faith of a new believer is daily transformed by the grace of God, it becomes the steadier, more decisive walk of a true disciple. This is our goal!*

Here are some challenging verses from Scripture, written in order to shake us out of any complacency:

If you faint in the day of adversity, your strength is small (Proverbs 24:10, ESV).

If you have raced with men on foot and they have worn you out, how can you compete with horses? If you stumble in safe country, how will you manage in the thickets by the Jordan? (Jeremiah 12:5, NIV).

Now, I would have thought that if I had fainted or faltered under severe pressure, it would have been because the pressure was too great, not because my strength was too small! But if these verses are true—which God's word always is—then we must get to work on strengthening our faith on a daily basis.

"Well," you might be thinking, "*work* doesn't sound like a whole load of fun to me!"

Here's what I mean by this:

Jesus told them, "This is the only work God wants from you: Believe in the one he has sent (John 6:29, NLT).

Take my yoke upon you and learn from me, for I am gentle and humble in heart, and you will find rest for your souls. For my yoke is easy and my burden is light (Matthew 11:29–30, NIV).

Dear friends, you always followed my instructions when I was with you. And now that I am away, it is even more important. Work hard to show the results of your salvation, obeying God with deep reverence and fear. For God is working in you, giving you the desire and the power to do what pleases him (Philippians 2:12–13, NLT).

Nobody wants to falter or fail, whether during times of trial or in day-to-day living. Instead, we all long to enjoy success in every area of our lives and to overcome life's toughest challenges! But what we sometimes forget is that, in order to succeed, we must fix our eyes on and seek God every step of the way, for He is the source of our strength.

> Only be strong and very courageous, being careful to do according to all the law that Moses my servant commanded you. Do not turn from it to the right hand or to the left, that you may have good success wherever you go (Joshua 1:7, ESV).

> Let us run with perseverance the race marked out for us, fixing our eyes on Jesus, the pioneer and perfecter of faith. For the joy set before him, he endured the cross, scorning its shame, and sat down at the right hand of the throne of God. Consider him who endured such opposition from sinners, so that you will not grow weary and lose heart (Hebrews 12:1–3, NIV).

Finally, I earlier touched on the truth that *faith is simple*. It is also the deepest source of spiritual power. "According to your faith let it be done to you" (Matthew 9:29, NIV).

So fully engage your faith to overcome life's challenges and maintain the victories that you have already won. My prayer is that everyone reading this book will receive and be strengthened by a renewed faith in God, knowing that His strength is all that we need. I strongly believe in offering hope and encouragement, both from God's word and from His moving in my own life. I trust that this discussion has been of some benefit to your personal faith and will help you recommit to maintaining your own unshakeable trust in God. May you be a light to the world!

God bless you.

Bukky Agboola

CPSIA information can be obtained
at www.ICGtesting.com
Printed in the USA
LVHW111451170522
719016LV00014B/82